Spoiler Alert!

Recent Releases from Open Court

Rick and Morty and Philosophy: In the Beginning Was the Squanch
Edited by Lester C. Abesamis and Wayne Yuen

Tom Petty and Philosophy: We Need to Know
Edited by Randall E. Auxier and Megan Volpert

WikiLeaking: The Ethics of Secrecy and Exposure
Edited by Christian Cotton and Robert Arp

1984 and Philosophy: Is Resistance Futile?
Edited by Ezio Di Nucci and Stefan Storrie

The Handmaid's Tale and Philosophy: A Womb of One's Own
Edited by Rachel Robison-Greene

Scott Adams and Philosophy: A Hole in the Fabric of Reality
Edited by Daniel Yim, Galen Foresman, and Robert Arp

For full details of all Open Court books, visit www.opencourtbooks.com.

Spoiler Alert!

(It's a Book about the Philosophy of Spoilers)

RICHARD GREENE

OPEN COURT
Chicago

To find out more about Open Court books, visit our website at www.opencourtbooks.com.

Open Court Publishing Company is a division of Carus Publishing Company, dba Cricket Media.

Copyright © 2019 by Carus Publishing Company, dba Cricket Media

First printing 2019

Printed and bound in the United States of America.

Spoiler Alert! It's a Book about the Philosophy of Spoilers

ISBN: 978-0-8126-9469-7

Library of Congress Control Number: 2019934548
This book is also available as an e-book (ISBN 978-0-8126-9473-4).

For Rachel Robison-Greene
who spoils me more than I deserve

Contents

Contents

Thanks

This book wouldn't have been possible without the support of my wife, Dr. Rachel Robison-Greene, with whom I've had countless wonderful philosophical conversations about pop culture in general and on the topic of spoilers in particular, my son, Henry, a weapons-grade level revealer of spoilers, the Department of Political Science and Philosophy at Weber State University (including dozens of students with whom I've discussed spoilers during classroom breaks and before and after class), David Ramsay Steele and the good folks at Open Court, Joe and Christina Charbonneau, whose insights about spoilers have made their way into this book in pretty significant form, Robert Arp, Patrick Croskery, Greg Spendlove, and Wayne Yuen, each of whom provided useful feedback on early versions of this book, the attendees at the 2017 and 2018 Salt Lake Comic Conventions (now known as "FanX"), the students and faculty members of the Philosophy Department at Harper College, who provided essential feed-back on early versions of some of the arguments contained in this book, my friends and colleagues at Charity Beyond Borders, who afforded me time to write and plenty of inspiration while traveling together in Ghana during June of 2018, The Shakespeare Room, the many who shared their spoiler horror stories with me, and of course all those jerks out there who love to spoil things for others, without whom this book would not be necessary or possible. I'm most grateful to each of you (albeit slightly less grateful to the jerks who love to spoil things for others).

A Few Words of Warning

Spoiler Alert!—this book is really good.

Also, this book contains quite a few spoilers. People talk about spoilers all the time. It seems that you don't go more than a few days without hearing the expression "Spoiler alert!" and you don't go much longer than that on average without hearing someone berate or admonish someone else for having spoiled something. Spoilers have become a huge part of contemporary culture, at least in those segments of society that pertain to popular culture and the Internet.

Spoilers also raise a number of interesting philosophical issues. What is a spoiler? What sorts of things can be spoiled? Is it bad to spoil something? If so, why is it bad? Is it ever okay to spoil something? Are movie trailers spoilers? Just to name a few. In the pages that follow, we will address all these questions and many more.

Naturally, this book will discuss the specifics of many of your favorite television shows, movies, novels, plays, and comic books. Not only is this necessary in order to give a thorough philosophical treatment of spoilers—one that conveys the full impact that spoilers can have and all their implications—it will also make the discussion a lot of fun! It's likely that you will already know most of the spoilers discussed (being the serious fan that you are!), but just in case you don't want to come across something that you would rather not see, I've included the following list, which lays out all the spoiler topics revealed in each chapter.[1] These topics are listed in the order in which they appear in the chapter, so you can choose where you want to stop reading (although my recommendation is that you simply watch all these movies and television programs and read all these books before you read any further, so that you won't miss anything).

So be sure to exercise the requisite caution as you delve within. You've been warned.

---

[1] Obviously, if I post the actual spoilers, anyone attempting to avoid spoilers by looking at the spoiler list, will necessarily see the spoilers. So instead, here I'll just list the titles of works that get spoiled in each chapter.

Spoilers Topics Revealed in This Book

Chapter 1

Voyage to the Bottom of the Sea
Oedipus the King
The Mousetrap
Les Diaboliques
Psycho
Happy Days
Mr. Roberts
A Simple Favor
Million Dollar Baby
Battlestar Galactica
Mad Men

Chapter 2

Lost in Space
Avengers: Infinity War
Harry Potter and the Half-Blood Prince
Wicked
Planet of the Apes
Night of the Living Dead
Game of Thrones
Star Wars: The Force Awakens
Star Wars: The Last Jedi

Chapter 3

The Empire Strikes Back
Harry Potter and the Half-Blood Prince
Planet of the Apes
The Simpsons
The Wizard of Oz
Avengers: Infinity War
Psycho
Murder on the Orient Express
Soylent Green
The Twilight Zone
Citizen Kane

Chapter 4

The Devil in the White City
American Horror Story

Chapter 5

Avengers: Infinity War
Ocean's 8
Star Wars: The Force Awakens
The Fault in our Stars
The Empire Strikes Back

Chapter 6

The Empire Strikes Back
Harry Potter and the Deathly Hallows
Harry Potter and the Half-Blood Prince
Red Sparrow
Psycho
Murder on the Orient Express
Better Call Saul

Chapter 7

The Usual Suspects
Game of Thrones
Old Yeller
Buffy the Vampire Slayer
Westworld
Twin Peaks
The Walking Dead

Chapter 8

Sharp Objects
The Man with Two Brains
Planet of the Apes
The Happytime Murders
Breaking Bad
Shameless
The Godfather: Part II
The Godfather
Ant-Man and the Wasp
Avengers: Infinity War

Chapter 9

Harry Potter and the Half-Blood Prince
The Revenant
Black Mirror
The Deer Hunter
A Quiet Place
Million Dollar Baby
Basic Instinct
Buffy the Vampire Slayer

Chapter 10

American Horror Story: Apocalypse
American Horror Story: Murder House

Chapter 11

Game Night
Psycho
Harry Potter and the Half-Blood Prince
Fight Club
Better Call Saul

Chapter 12

The Princess Bride
Murder on the Orient Express
Step Brothers
Monty Python's The Meaning of Life
National Lampoon's Christmas Vacation
The Sixth Sense
The Usual Suspects
Fight Club
Bad Times at the El Royale
Psycho
Planet of the Apes
The Empire Strikes Back
Westworld

Chapter 13

Murder on the Orient Express
The Empire Strikes Back
Psycho
Planet of the Apes
Harry Potter and the Half-Blood Prince

Chapter 13 (cont'd)

The Twilight Zone
Psycho (1998 version)
Planet of the Apes (2001 version)
Pride and Prejudice (1940, 1995, and 2005 versions)
Avengers: Infinity War
Eternal Sunshine of the Spotless Mind
Yogi Bear
Plan 9 from Outer Space
The Room

Chapter 14

Halloween
Shutter Island
Carnival of Souls

Chapter 15

Voyage to the Bottom of the Sea

Chapter 16

Harry Potter and the Half-Blood Prince
Psycho
Planet of the Apes

The Lists (Appendixes 1, 2, and 3)

Too many spoilers to mention! If you don't want to
encounter spoilers, just skip these parts,

I

The Metaphysics of Spoilers

1

A Brief History
of Spoilers

1966 was a great year for movies, especially if you were a five-year-old kid. Among the dozens of films that were released that year were *Fantastic Voyage, Dracula: Prince of Darkness, Django, Batman, Godzilla vs. the Sea Monster, The Witches, Our Man Flint, The Ghost in the Invisible Bikini, Stagecoach,* and my personal favorite *The Ghost and Mr. Chicken.*

One thing that each of these movies had in common (besides all being really great movies!) is that I knew what was going to happen in each one before I saw it—every twist, every ending, and every gruesome attack!

Back then my friends and I would race to be the one to reveal a spoiler to the entire group, though we didn't think of them as spoilers. It was a kind of competition among us: "Did you see *Voyage to the Bottom of the Sea* this week? The Seaview was attacked by a werewolf!" Surprisingly, no one would have dreamed of objecting upon hearing this news. We simply didn't have the concept of a spoiler. Perhaps the rules were different for kids back then.[1] My

---

[1] Things have certainly changed. When my son was five we would take him to see his favorite movies. Sometimes we would go several times to the same film. True to form (being the master of spoilers that he is), he would narrate what was about to happen next during the entire film (despite our

parents didn't have the concept of a spoiler in 1966 either, but I'm fairly certain that had someone blurted out the ending of a good whodunit as they were entering our local movie house, they would have been pretty darned annoyed.

Still, things weren't the same back then as they are today with respect to spoilers, even for adults. That sort of transgression nowadays would likely generate some real ire (especially if it had to do with the plot of a much-anticipated release, such as the latest installment in either the *Star Wars* or Marvel Cinematic Universe franchises). People would not just be perturbed, they would be downright furious. On more than one occasion I've seen someone either publicly shamed or berated for revealing a spoiler while exiting the theater. It is virtually impossible to overstate the extent to which there exists a greater prohibition on revealing spoilers today than was in place fifty years ago. Spoiling is something you simply don't do nowadays.

There's a useful distinction to be made between having a concept (for example, the concept of a spoiler) and the thing that the concept is a concept of (for example, spoilers) actually existing. While we didn't have the concept of a spoiler back in the 1960s, spoilers certainly existed. In fact, spoilers have existed for about as long as there have been things to spoil. We can easily imagine, for example, some citizen of Athens in 429 B.C.E. leaving the Theater of Dionysus on the opening night of Sophocles's *Oedipus the King* shouting "OMG, Oedipus slept with his own mother!" (or something along those lines). This can't be verified, but it would be shocking if things like this didn't happen

---

constant admonishments). The other kids (and some parents) would be furious with him. Eventually he grew out of it, but not before spoiling what must be well into the hundreds of key plot points.

(there have been jerks for considerably longer than there have been things to spoil). There is an interesting question as to just what can be spoiled, which we will get to a little later, but in the meantime, we're going to look at the history of spoilers, which for our purposes is the history of the concept of the spoiler. Specifically, when did people begin to think about spoilers as such, and when did it become such a bad thing to spoil?

When Did Spoilers Become Spoilers?

As I've suggested, folks didn't used to react to spoilers the way they do now, and part of the reason for this is that they didn't conceive of spoilers in the same way. It seems that the modern conception of the spoiler came about overnight, and in the grand scheme of things it did, but the development of the concept of a spoiler was something that occurred somewhat gradually over the past sixty-five or so years.

A good place to start is with Agatha Christie's 1952 play *The Mousetrap*. At the end of each performance (a tradition that continues today!), the audience was admonished to not reveal the ending.[2] Similar admonitions came at the end of the 1955 French film *Les Diaboliques* and Alfred Hitchcock's 1960 classic film *Psycho*.[3,4,5] While the term "spoiler" was not yet being used, the concept was well on its way. The producers of these shows believed that

---

[2] <https://literature.stackexchange.com/questions/2536/history-of-spoilers>.

[3] Ibid.

[4] <http://www.bbc.co.uk/newsbeat/article/36128869/a-brief-history-of-film-and-tv-spoilers-as-game-of-thrones-returns>.

[5] Apparently, not everyone got the memo on *Les Diaboliques*. The movie *A Simple Favor*, which can be seen as an homage to *Les Diaboliques*, reveals a pretty significant spoiler about the film.

telling folks the surprise endings or other plot twists would somehow spoil the experience for them. There is a healthy debate to be had over whether that is in fact true, which we will have a little later in the book.

The term "spoiler" first appears in print in 1971. It was in an article in *National Lampoon* magazine entitled "Spoilers."[6,7] The author, Doug Kenney, who was the founder of *National Lampoon* as well as the writer of *Caddyshack* and one of the writers of *Animal House*, restricted the term "spoilers" to trick endings to novels and movies.[8] In this tongue-in-cheek article he spoils the endings to a number of movies, including *Citizen Kane*, *The Birds*, *The Godfather*, and *Psycho* (just to name a few). He also spoils the endings of a number of Agatha Christie novels. This was done as a service to readers "in order to save people time and money."

While Kenney was just trying to be funny, by introducing the term "spoiler" he did, in fact, do folks a real service. Our concept of a spoiler was starting to become solidified. That said, it hadn't solidified yet. In 1976 on an episode of *Happy Days* ("Fonzie the Superstar") Howard Cunningham tells Ralph Malph that they are going to see *Psycho*. Ralph exclaims "What an ending! Tony Perkins is his own mother." This causes the Cunninghams to change their movie plans to *Mr. Roberts*, which Ralph also spoils for them (Mr. Roberts dies!). So, in 1976 we are starting to realize that spoiling is bad (or at least has bad consequences), but we are not yet feeling the force of the prohibition against spoiling that we are well aware of today. Otherwise, the producers of *Happy Days* would not

---

[6] <https://en.wikipedia.org/wiki/Spoiler_(media)>.

[7] <https://www.visualthesaurus.com/cm/wordroutes/spoiler-alert-revealing-the-origins-of-the-spoiler>.

[8] <https://www.techtimes.com/articles/117575/20151218/when-national-lampoon-magazine-dropped-atom-bomb-spoilers.htm>.

have felt it appropriate to spoil *Psycho* for the millions of viewers who tuned in for that episode.

The first digital spoiler warning appears in 1979, although it doesn't involve the term "spoiler alert."[9] The moderator of a mailing list hosted by MIT called "SF-Lovers" (for science fiction lovers, and not lovers of San Francisco) posted spoiler warnings on emails that discussed the first *Star Trek* movie. The first use of the term "spoiler alert" occurred in 1982 on a Usenet news group. It also pertained to an entry in the *Star Trek* movie franchise: *The Wrath of Khan*.[10] Clearly the Treksters[11] like to be out in front these things. By 1994 the use of the term "spoiler alert" is somewhat widespread on Internet discussion pages, but had not made its way into the consciousness of those who were not on the cutting edge of Internet technology.[12] It wasn't until 2000 that the term "spoiler alert" became commonplace across the Internet (and not just on discussion pages), and it was at least a few years after that it became commonplace in non-Internet forums. For example, the first appearance of the term "spoiler alert" in the *New York Times* does not appear until 2002.[13]

From there four things happened to bring the concept of the spoiler from where it was fifty or sixty years ago (virtually non-existent) to where it is today (a concept that nearly everyone living in North America or Europe could

---

[9] <https://www.visualthesaurus.com/cm/wordroutes/spoiler-alert-revealing-the-origins-of-the-spoiler>.

[10] Ibid.

[11] I realize that no one other than me calls them "Treksters," but I'd really like to avoid the whole Trekkies vs. Trekkers debate, which just might go down in history at the stupidest intra-fandom debate ever.

[12] <https://www.theawl.com/2010/07/the-history-and-use-of-spoiler-alert>.

[13] <https://www.nytimes.com/2002/06/17/arts/television-review-you-never-know-when-you-ll-find-a-good-idea.html>.

not have failed to have heard or used). First, the Internet ceased to be something that only a small percentage of folks had exposure to. It rapidly became common for every home to have multiple means of accessing the Internet, whether it be via a computer or an early smartphone (and later tablets, e-readers, and so forth). Second, the term "spoiler alert" on the Internet was no longer confined to chat rooms and discussion boards. The rise of social media and the increase in personal webpages and blogs propagated the use of the term greatly. Not surprisingly, this corresponded to a vast increase in the number of spoilers, as well. As it became easier for people to spoil things, spoiler alerts became much more ubiquitous, and became necessary with greater regularity. Third, the term "spoiler alert" began to make its way into common conversation. It's now to the point where "spoiler alert" is not only being used in its legitimate sense (to warn people about spoilers), but it has also taken on a metaphorical and sometimes ironic use, often used to foreshadow things people are just about to say, even when someone's knowing those things in advance would not spoil anything for them. "Spoiler Alert! We are having pot roast for dinner." "Spoiler Alert! You are grounded!" "Spoiler Alert! The Lakers are going to be good this year." You get the idea.[14] Finally, in early 2019 the first comprehensive book on the philosophy of spoilers was published.[15]

---

[14] When I was three or four years old I "spoiled" my father's birthday present. We had purchased a transistor radio for him. He was to open it after supper. During our meal I exclaimed "I want a radio just like Dad's." This sort of thing today would be undoubtedly followed by people yelling "Spoiler Alert!" even though this is not actually a spoiler as the term gets defined.

[15] *Spoiler Alert! (It's a Book about the Philosophy of Spoilers)*, Richard Greene (Chicago: Open Court).

When Did It Become Such a Bad Thing to Spoil?

In 2011 a study came out of the University of California, San Diego. The study, which was summarized for the public at large in a *Wired* magazine article, argued that knowing spoilers doesn't diminish one's enjoyment of a particular work.[16] We'll consider this claim further in Chapter 6, but regardless of whether the results of this study are correct, people undoubtedly consider spoilers to be a bad thing—and in certain circles, they are considered to be a very bad thing. As I mentioned previously, this was not always the case. Some folks likely would have had a negative reaction upon having something spoiled for them fifty years ago, but that would not have been the norm. Spoilers were, to some extent, a fact of life, and they tended to not bother people much. This raises the question of when it became such a bad thing to spoil. Or, at minimum, it raises the question of when people began to consider it bad to spoil something.

It makes sense that to the extent that folks are not in possession of a particular concept that they wouldn't have opinions about the goodness or badness of that concept. Of course, fifty years ago no one considered spoilers to be a bad thing. People just weren't thinking about spoilers. It also makes sense that as people become more aware of a particular concept, they are more apt to form attitudes about that concept. So, one would expect that as awareness of spoilers spread, the existence of strong feelings about the badness of spoilers would also spread—more people are likely to be bothered by spoilers, if more people have the concept of spoilers. That said, the changes over the last fifty or so years in people's attitudes about spoilers do not map perfectly onto people's awareness of

---

[16] <https://www.wired.com/2011/08/spoilers-dont-spoil-anything>.

spoilers over the same period of time. This is due to a handful of significant events.

A couple of these events involved changes to our viewing habits. In 1999 TiVO and ReplayTV marketed the first digital video recorders (DVRs). This allowed people to record programs as they aired and watch them at their convenience. There had been Video Cassette Recorders (VCRs) for decades at this point, but they tended to be of comparatively poor quality and cumbersome to use, and did not affect the viewing habits of many people (lots of households had them, few used them to record programs). Prior to the introduction of DVRs, if you didn't watch something when it first aired, you generally missed it (or had to wait for several months for the program to be re-aired).[17] As a consequence, there didn't exist much of a prohibition against discussing spoilers of television programs after their original air date. As folks began watching things on a different and elongated schedule—sometimes not for weeks after the original airing—it became increasingly likely that discussions of those programs (especially in public forums) would serve to spoil things. People's frustration with having things spoiled also increased. In part, this was due to the fact that not only had someone not seen a particular thing at the point that it was spoiled for them, they had also exerted energy (they took the time necessary to program their DVR) to ensure that they would not miss it, and in a great number of cases, took steps to ensure that they would not have it spoiled. It's no wonder that people became increasingly agitated and increasing intolerant of spoilers.

---

[17] At the time, premium cable networks, such as HBO, constituted a counterexample to this general claim, as they aired their programs multiple times per week. Still, most viewers were watching HBO original programming at the time it originally aired.

A second change to people's viewing habits came about in 2007 when Netflix began offering streaming services. This allowed people to stream programs, an entire season (or more!) at a time, without it clogging up their limited DVR space (the first DVRs didn't have much storage, so folks had to be pretty choosy about what they saved). The era of binge-watching programs was upon us. The effect of this is that many folks would wait until an entire season of a particular program is released on Netflix (or on one of the other streaming formats) before watching it. Often, even with very popular programs, such as *Breaking Bad*, it took around one year for programs to appear on certain streaming services. People began to demand that folks refrain from spoiling things until after they've had opportunity to stream them, and even though the wait was longer, the level of vitriol and animosity expressed toward those who would reveal spoilers continued to rise.

Perhaps the single most significant event in the evolution of people's attitudes regarding the badness of spoilers occurred in 2005 when popular film critic Roger Ebert of the *Chicago Sun-Times* wrote a column admonishing other reviewers to not include spoilers in their reviews without including the appropriate spoiler warnings.[18] In this article his comments are directed at all film reviewers, in general, arguing that they don't have the right to spoil surprises that *they* were allowed to react to in an unspoiled fashion, but his comments are also directed specifically at conservative commentators Rush Limbaugh and Michael Medved (Medved , by the way, was formerly a movie critic) who had revealed spoilers about the film *Million Dollar Baby* because they disagreed with the movie's message regarding

---

[18] Roger Ebert (2005-01-29). "Critics Have No Right to Play Spoiler." *Chicago Sun-Times*. Retrieved 2016-01-28.

the morality of euthanasia.[19] In the article, Ebert vowed to always issue spoiler warnings moving forward. Ebert's article went viral and was widely discussed in the media and talk radio. While some sided with Limbaugh and Medved on this issue, most folks came away from the discussion with a considerably stronger sense of the badness of spoiling.

If the Ebert article marks the most significant single event regarding our attitudes toward spoilers, right on its heels are a number of well-publicized reveals that went viral due to the outrage of various fandoms. One such instance occurred in 2009 when the *Los Angeles Times* published a story containing spoilers from the previous night's episode of *Battlestar Galactica*—that Ellen Tigh is the fifth Cylon!—without issuing a spoiler warning.[20] This led to quite a bit of discussion in both editorial pages and on the Internet about just how long you must wait before posting spoilers. What is noteworthy about this is there wasn't much discussion of whether it is wrong to reveal spoilers; the badness of spoilers by this time was already being assumed—we had crossed some sort of threshold.

The *Los Angeles Times / Battlestar Galactica* ordeal pales in comparison to what is still considered by many to be the most egregious spoiler reveal ever: The *Mad Men* spoiler reveal of 2010. Allesandra Stanley, television critic for the *New York Times*, revealed a significant detail about the Season Four premiere of *Mad Men* without issuing a

---

[19] It turns out that not everyone got Limbaugh's and Medved's message. I was in San Antonio Texas with a debate team that I was coaching when *Million Dollar Baby* was in the theaters. Our team didn't fare well at this particular competition, and the students were a little depressed, so I decided to take them to the movies. My words still echo in my head "Let's go to that boxing movie; boxing movies are always uplifting." Ugh! Sorry kids!

[20] <http://blogs.sun-sentinel.com/tv/2009/01/how-soon-is-too-soon-for-spoilers.html>.

spoiler warning.[21] Unsuspecting fans of the show read her article only to find out that Don and Betty Draper were divorced (a possibility that was hinted at in the Season Three finale, but not confirmed until the Season Four premiere). The fans were furious, but it does not end there. The producers of *Mad Men*, including show creator Matthew Weiner, were livid. The story went viral. The Internet was abuzz, as were the trade magazines. The rage against Stanley was nearly universal.

The *Mad Men* affair served to reinforce in nearly everyone's mind that spoilers without warnings were unacceptable, those who spoil deserve to be publicly shamed (or worse!), and that spoilers themselves were really bad. With little exception, these attitudes have not changed or subsided much since 2010. If anything, people tend to feel even more strongly today about the badness of spoilers than ever before. Subsequently, the production companies that make today's movies and television programs have gone to greater lengths to protect their secrets. They routinely implore film critics not to reveal important information (even, on occasion, highlighting things they would like to not be revealed), and occasionally engage in misinformation campaigns. The media has played a role in stopping the release of spoilers, as well. For example, there is no shortage of spoiler etiquette guides to be found online (which we will look at in Chapter 10).

So that's how we got here: a handful of chance events combined with the power of the Internet and streaming technology, and a couple of well-timed articles, has left us in such a mental state that we become downright furious when we encounter spoilers, and has collectively positioned us to bring swift justice in many cases to those who

---

[21] <https://variety.com/2010/voices/opinion/stanley-gives-mad-men-fans-reason-to-get-mad-4348>.

spoil. Generally speaking, swift justice comes in the form a public shaming or a stern admonition. Occasionally, swift justice is something considerably more severe. On October 9th 2018 Sergei Savitsky, a Russian electrical engineer who was doing research on a remote island in Antarctica (pretty much everything in Antarctica is remote) stabbed Oleg Beloguvoz, a welder, with whom Savitsky had been isolated for some time, several times in the chest with a knife for continually revealing the endings of books that Savitsky had been reading.[22] This is a very far cry from where we started. Let's turn our attention now to the nature of spoilers.

---

[22]   <http://www.latimes.com/books/la-et-jc-anarctica-stabbing-books-20181030-story.html?fbclid=IwAR2h3nagltF67p6_gHjeeM9Btq-daQGdc0cpHFVG0Miz2SME2ohE_cAVQpjs>.

2
What Are Spoilers?

First things first. Before we get into some of the really thorny issues pertaining to spoilers, it will prove useful to get clear on just what constitutes a spoiler, which, as we will see, is a pretty thorny issue in its own right.

When discussing spoilers with various groups of people, such as my students or fans of a particular show, movie, or comic book, it soon becomes apparent that there is quite a bit of agreement about whether or not some bit of information is a spoiler. This doesn't mean that there is much agreement over how to define a spoiler, nor does it mean that there is much agreement about what sorts of things can be spoiled (at least not when spoilers are raised as a philosophical concept); rather, it just means that if I ask people whether such and such is a spoiler, they will all mostly say the same thing. It's sort of like Supreme Court Justice Stewart Potter's famous statement on obscenity: "I don't know how to define it, but I know what it is when I see it." People have a strong intuitive sense of what constitutes a spoiler. We will use this intuitive sense as a launching point as we attempt to offer a philosophical definition of spoilers. We can use our intuitions here as a measuring stick for whether our account is working. If our definition moves too far away from what people intuitively and pretheoretically consider to be a spoiler, then we will know that something in our definition has failed.[1] One of the chief projects of this chapter is to give a philosophical account of spoilers that explains and elucidates our ordinary usage of the term.[2] Hence our intuitions about spoilers and common usage of the term "spoilers" play a central role in our doing so.

Related to this is the fact that there are a great many clear-cut paradigmatic cases of spoilers. Suppose, for example, a friend tells me that he just started watching the reboot of *Lost in Space* on Netflix, and I respond by telling him that towards the end of Season One Dr. Smith gains control of Will Robinson's robot. Pretty much everyone would consider this to be a spoiler. Similarly, were I to tell him that a bunch of his favorite Marvel characters die at the end of *Avengers: Infinity War*, that would also constitute a spoiler.

These examples have something in common, namely, that in each case information about a television show or movie is revealed.

So, as a first attempt, let's define a spoiler as follows.

(SP1): A spoiler is any information about the plot of a television show or movie (distinct from that television show or movie itself)

---

[1] What I have in mind here is what ethicists commonly refer to as the "method of reflective equilibrium" in which an equilibrium is struck between our pretheoretical intuitions and what our theory hypothesizes.

[2] This is not to suggest that everyone, or even all native speakers of English, are using the term "spoiler" in the same way. Nor is it to suggest that everyone, or even all native speakers of English, have the same intuitions about what counts as a spoiler. For example, English is the official language of Ghana, but in discussing these issues with Ghanaians, it became clear that they typically don't share the same intuitions as do folks in most English-speaking Western nations.

that has the potential to reveal information to someone who has not yet encountered that information.[3,4]

An essential part of this definition is the *potential* revealing of information, as opposed to the *actual* revealing of information. Not every spoiler actually spoils. Consider my friend Cassandra (this is not her real name, but I strongly suspect that she knows who I'm talking about here) who frequently posts the pictures of characters on *The Walking Dead* on her Facebook wall immediately after the episode in which they die is aired in her time zone (often before the episode has had a chance to air in all time zones). When she does this, she is posting spoilers. Even if it turns out on some occasion that the only people who see it are people who have already seen the episode or already had that information spoiled for them (seriously, people, STOP POSTING SPOILERS ON SOCIAL MEDIA!!!). So, something is a spoiler in virtue of its ability to spoil, and not in virtue of its actually spoiling something.

This is not to say that there is not a legitimate and real connection between something's being a spoiler and its effect on things in the real world (spoilers are not merely abstract entities that exist in some non-worldly realm as do Platonic forms). Consider a case in which I drive fifty

---

[3] The parenthetical "distinct from that television show or movie" clause is required. Otherwise the shows and movies themselves would count as spoilers, as they reveal information to those who have not previously encountered it.

[4] To all intents and purposes, you cannot spoil something for someone who has previously encountered that thing. For convenience's sake we'll treat all spoilers as though they require new information, even though we can imagine cases in which someone has encountered the spoiled information previously (for instance, someone who has watched a movie and subsequently experienced complete and irreversible memory loss, such that seeing the same movie would be identical to a first viewing in all relevant respects).

miles out into the desert, miles from the nearest person, and shout "Thanos Killed Star-Lord." This, of course, would not count as a spoiler, even though in other contexts (such as were it to appear in this book) it would count as a spoiler. The right thing to say about this case is that uttering would-be spoilers in contexts in which it is certain that nobody will hear them lacks the ability to spoil anything, and for that reason doing so fails to be a spoiler. Again, the idea of a spoiler having the potential to reveal something is essential. So, according to this view stating a would-be spoiler is a necessary condition, but not a sufficient condition for something's being a spoiler.

One question that arises has to do with the meaning of the term "reveal." It's not the case that any utterance of a spoiler in contexts in which someone might hear it counts as a spoiler, either. Suppose, for example, that I have no idea what happens in a particular film, but on the way in to the cinema I jokingly say to a friend, the killer is the husband. If it turns out to be true that the killer is the husband, we wouldn't want to say that I revealed a spoiler, since I didn't know that it was true at the time that I said it (and my friend knew that I wasn't seriously claiming to know). So, we will henceforth restrict our use of the term "reveal" to those cases in which the revealer of potential information is actually in possession of that information.

Revising Our Account

The virtue of our current definition (SP1) is that it pretty much captures most instances of spoilers, and it seems to be what most people have in mind when they talk or fret or vent about spoilers. That said, this account does not withstand even the slightest scrutiny. For example, it's not just television shows and movies that can be spoiled. Were someone to reveal that in the sixth book of the *Harry Pot-*

ter series Snape killed Dumbledore, they certainly would have spoiled it for that person. Similarly, if I were to reveal that in the play *Wicked* Elphaba essentially fakes her own death, I would be spoiling the surprise ending for others. So, this leads us to a revised definition of spoilers—one that can account for the fact that spoilers are not limited to television shows and movies.

> (SP2): A spoiler is any information about a work of fiction (distinct from that work of fiction itself), including plays, novels, television programs, movies, that has the potential to reveal information to someone who has not yet encountered that information.

Spoilers and Significance

(SP2) is an improvement on our first definition, but it, too, is not without its shortcomings. For example, if I were to tell my friend that the Robinson Family deals with some tough situations in the reboot of *Lost in Space*, most people would not consider this to be a spoiler, but it satisfies the requirements of our second definition.

Why does the information about Dr. Smith gaining control of Will Robinson's robot count as a spoiler but not the information about the Robinsons' dealing with tough situations? It is because the former reveals something significant, whereas the latter does not. As fans of the original series know well, Dr. Smith coveted Will Robinson's relationship with the robot, and her having control of the robot, constitutes a major plot point. In the second example, while many of the predicaments that the Robinsons find themselves in could aptly be described as tough situations, knowing that doesn't count as a spoiler, as there is nothing shocking about coming to possess that knowledge. In fact, it's just the opposite: one would expect nothing less from a show called *Lost in Space* than to have the family that is lost find themselves in tough predicaments (it would be pretty boring otherwise).

This leads to our third definition:

(SP3): A spoiler is any information about a work of fiction (distinct from that work of fiction itself), including plays, novels, television programs, movies, that has the potential to reveal some significant (or shocking) information to someone who has not yet encountered that information.

There are a couple of things to note about this definition. First, the idea of something being significant or potentially shocking is pretty intuitive, but needs to be spelled out a bit further. Suppose that a new *Star Trek* movie is released and someone decides to post on social media that there is a Vulcan in it. This, I should think, would not count as significant in the sense intended in our current definition, since pretty much all *Star Trek* movies have Vulcans in them.[5] On another interpretation of the information, however, it would count as significant to the extent that in most *Star Trek* movies, Vulcans play pretty significant roles. Our concern is significance in the first sense.

Second, it's worth noting that nothing in this definition restricts the class of spoilers to plot points. Any variety of things beyond plot points could serve as spoilers. Let's address each of these in turn.

Significance is a tricky concept for a number of reasons. First, it's a pretty vague concept. Significance admits of degrees. Consider a few examples from the original

---

[5] Of course, we could imagine a situation where this sort of information would count as significant. Suppose that the movie studio went out of their way to get people to believe that no Vulcans would appear in the movie, only to have a surprise appearance by Mr. Spock. But putting those sorts of cases aside, the example stands.

Planet of the Apes. That there was a hunt in which the apes hunted humans is a significant plot point, but, as far as spoilers go, it's not as significant as the fact that Zira befriended Taylor and helped him escape. Why is the latter more significant than the former? It can't be how essential each is to the plot, because had the hunt not happened, then the befriending would not have happened—the hunt constitutes a pretty major event in the film. Rather, it has something to do with which is more integral to the story being a good story. This can cash out in a number of ways, but in *Planet of the Apes* one of the things that is special about the film is Zira's relationship with Taylor, and the statement that the film was making about prejudice and superficial or irrelevant features being used to determine who has value and who should be afforded the highest rights in a society.

Moreover, if we knew going into the movie that there was going to be a hunt, it's likely that our enjoyment of the film (and the hunt scene in particular) would not be diminished much at all. It's sort of like going to a Michael Bay movie with the foreknowledge that things will get blown up. On the other hand, knowing that Zira is going to help Taylor escape in advance would serve to eliminate a lot of the tension in the film, during the scenes where Taylor is imprisoned. I recall wondering when I first watched *Planet of the Apes* "How is he going to get out of this?" I was on the edge of my seat the entire time. I certainly would not have enjoyed the film as much had I known how it would play out.

Similarly, that the planet of the apes turns out to be a post-apocalyptic earth, is more significant than the fact that Zira befriends Taylor and helps him escape. The former is both the payoff of the movie and a surprise ending. As Taylor gazed upon the ruins of the Statue of Liberty and screamed "You Maniacs! You blew it up! Oh, damn you! Goddamn you all to Hell!" audiences were stunned. At once the entire meaning of the movie changed. It went from being primarily a movie about prejudice and arbitrariness to being a movie about humanity's ultimate destruction (along with prejudice and arbitrariness, of course). It was a perfect ending to the film, and would have been less than perfect had the audience seen it coming.

So, roughly, we can conclude that significance is tied to the viewer's experience. Those spoilers, were they revealed to a typical viewer or reader, that would more greatly diminish that viewer's experience upon first encountering the work in question are considered to be more significant spoilers. Similarly, those spoilers that would less greatly diminish that viewer's experience, are considered to be less significant spoilers.

Second, people don't always agree on what counts as significant (in the sense intended in our definition). This actually can be broken down into two separate concerns. There are certain plot points that no one would dispute as being of the highest significance. Major plot twists, surprise endings, the answer to the question "Who dunnit?", and so forth, all fall into this category. With events of lesser significance, however, there is much disagreement. We could easily imagine a healthy debate between fans of George A. Romero's *Night of the Living Dead* who essentially agree on what they most like to see in a horror movie (their aesthetic values line up perfectly) discussing whether the explanation for how zombies came into existence as proffered by the film is a more significant part of the film than the backstory that explains why Barbara and John Blair were hanging out in a graveyard when the living dead begin to attack. So, a disagreement about the significance of certain plot points, and ultimately, a disagreement about the significance of particular spoilers, need not entail a disagreement in values. Conversely, two fans could have entirely different values, such that upon reading the *Harry Potter* series one could place great significance on Harry's relationship with Hagrid, even considering it to be one of the payoffs of the series, while another might think that Harry's relationship with Dumbledore is of higher significance.

It will be useful here to introduce a distinction between what we can call "personal spoilers" and what we can call "impersonal spoilers." A personal spoiler is something that is generally not a spoiler for others (or is not a particularly significant spoiler for others), but has the effect of being a spoiler for a particular person or a small group of persons. An impersonal spoiler is what we normally consider to be a spoiler—it's what we've been talking about all along, namely, our common-sense notion of a spoiler. For the most part, this book is about impersonal spoilers, so when we merely say "spoiler" we will mean "impersonal spoiler." We will, however, have plenty of occasion to discuss personal spoilers.

The rules for personal spoilers are pretty simple. If something is not generally considered to be a legitimate spoiler (that is, among other things, a spoiler in the impersonal sense), but someone who does not have that information would be adversely affected by receiving it (they would be pissed off, bummed out, their mellow would be harshed, they would have a diminished experienced when they get around to viewing the show or movie), then don't reveal it. Again, it's simply a matter of not being a jerk.[6]

With this distinction in mind, let's return to our discussion of significance. Our current definition (SP3) requires that a spoiler have the ability to reveal something that is significant. Given that significance admits of degrees and people place different significance on different

---

[5] This is good advice in general, which doesn't pertain only to spoilers.

things, there is not a straightforward way to distinguish significant information and insignificant information that will apply in all cases. Thus, it becomes necessary to appropriate what I call a "typical viewer" standard. Here the right thing to ask is whether a typical fan of a particular work would consider the information significant. Admittedly this is a pretty crude and imprecise measure for when something counts as significant, but it serves to distinguish the most clear-cut cases (for example, this standard will distinguish the "Dr. Smith gains control of Will Robinson's robot" cases from "The Robinsons find themselves in tough predicaments" cases). This, for our purposes is sufficient, as the personal spoiler/impersonal spoiler distinction can capture the tougher cases. Suppose, for example, that it's not entirely clear whether a typical viewer will consider some bit of information to be significant. One can always ask whether the particular people that will come across that information might consider it to be significant. When we discuss the ethics of spoilers (a little later in the book) we will see that either way, if someone one might consider the information to be a spoiler, we should refrain from disseminating it.

Recall that previously we said that our current definition (SP3) does nothing to restrict the class of spoilers to plot points. This is a virtue of this definition, as it's not just plot points that constitute spoilers. For example, at the end of Season Five of *Game of Thrones* Jon Snow is killed at the hands of his own men. Fans of the television show (at least those who had not been reading the book) were shocked and in disbelief. There was much speculation as to whether Jon Snow was really dead, whether he would remain dead, whether he would still be on the show (perhaps only in flashbacks), and so on. Speculation is fine and does not in and of itself constitute a spoiler, but bit by bit the speculation was combined with pertinent information about the upcoming season. There was information that placed Kit Harrington (the actor who plays Jon Snow) on set with certain other actors and in particular locations. Savvy fans of the show had no trouble deducing that Jon Snow would be brought back to life and his quest would continue. This information was all over the Internet (I'm looking at you, in particular, Reddit).

A similar thing happened just before Season 7 of *Game of Thrones* when information about where Emilia Clarke, who plays Daenerys Targaryen, was filming was leaked. Since *Game of Thrones* is filmed in a number of distinct locations, location information allows us to readily deduce plot information. In this case it was revealed that not only would Daenerys first arrive at Westeros at her ancestral home, Dragonstone, but that she would first meet Jon Snow there.

This sort of thing is not just limited to *Game of Thrones*. Famously, in 2015 just a few months prior to the release of *Star Wars: The Force Awakens* Mark Hamill tweeted about his beard being long enough to begin filming Episode VIII (later titled *Star Wars: The Last Jedi*). This allowed fans to deduce that Hamill's character, Luke Skywalker, was not killed in *The Force Awakens* (at the time there was much speculation about Luke Skywalker's fate).

So, it's not just specific information about the plot that constitutes a spoiler, it can be information about a wide array of things from actors, to locations, to props, and so on. This also illustrates another key point about spoilers. You might think that in order to spoil something, you must have either viewed that thing for yourself or passed along a spoiler that you heard from some other source, but that is not right. You can spoil something just by passing along some critical information about a production that you have not yet seen.

Taking stock, thus far SP3 is looking pretty good. It captures our intuitive sense of the term "spoiler" as it is used in the common vernacular, and it makes explicit that spoilers must involve information that is significant or potentially shocking. There are, however, a few wrinkles to be addressed.

Suppose that the Mrs. and I are watching an episode of *The Tudors*, and I remark to her that Anne Boleyn gets beheaded. This I consider to not be a spoiler. Why not? Because it is common knowledge that Anne Boleyn gets beheaded.[7] Similarly, if we were about to watch the film *Vesuvius* (I don't believe that I'm spoiling anything when I say it is not the aforementioned Kit Harrington's finest work) and I report that a volcano is going to erupt, I've not spoiled anything. One might object that it would be a spoiler if my wife had never heard of Anne Boleyn or Mount Vesuvius. Here our distinction between personal and impersonal spoilers comes into play. Since common knowledge is intimately tied to the typical viewer standard (if a typical viewer would know it, it counts as common knowledge), the revealing of common knowledge in the context of viewing something doesn't count as a spoiler (in the impersonal sense), but may count as a personal spoiler (in which case, one shouldn't reveal the information).[8]

---

[7] Things can get a bit tricky in cases such as these, as it may not be common knowledge that Anne Boleyn gets beheaded in the particular episode that we are currently watching, in which case we may be back in the spoiler business, after all.

[8] I'm somewhat open to the idea that since typical viewers are defined as typical fans of some work of fiction and common knowledge is more appropriately based on what a typical person in a given culture would know, it is possible for the concepts to cleave to some degree. We can consider the small subset of cases in which they don't map perfectly on one another as special, and take them on a case by case basis, as to whether they count as spoilers (in the impersonal sense).

Related to this is the idea that we cannot spoil something that is too, shall we say, "out there." That is, one can't spoil something that is too much a part of the public consciousness. This is similar to common knowledge, but rather than involving knowledge of events, it involves knowledge of concepts or, perhaps, of particular story lines or tropes, and the like. (Admittedly, this is a bit of a catch-all category.) A great example of this is the main conceit of the book and subsequent film *Catch-22*. The idea of a Catch-22—an undesirable circumstance that one might find oneself in, such that any attempt to get out of it is thwarted by features of that very attempt—has become part of our common language. Nearly everyone knows what a Catch-22 is, such that to tell that there is one in the book, couldn't possibly count as significant or potentially shocking. Similarly, suppose that there is a new production of *Romeo and Juliet*. It would not count as a spoiler to reveal to someone that the star-crossed lovers both die in the end, as everyone knows that is what is going to happen. Again, there is always the possibility of revealing a personal spoiler to someone who has never seen *Romeo and Juliet,* but that, as we've seen, is a different matter. For convenience I'll lump this category in with common knowledge.

Timing and Spoilers

Timing is an issue that is relevant to whether something counts as a spoiler. We've already seen that if you're revealing non-spoiling information to someone for whom that information might be a personal spoiler, you ought not to reveal that information (for example, you ought not tell someone who has a pretty sketchy knowledge of world history and is about to watch a movie about World War II that the Germans lose).

Timing is important in another sense. Spoilers have a shelf life. Generally speaking, you cannot spoil something that is too old. Suppose that I've recently watched an episode of *The Mary Tyler Moore Show*, and in recounting the episode to some friends I reveal that Sue Ann Nivens has a torrid fling with Chuckles the Clown. They may not be aware of this, but it would hardly count as a spoiler, as the episode aired about forty years ago.[9] The point is that spoilers have a shelf life and, generally speaking, it's considerably less than forty years. Since people enjoy talking about things they've viewed, it is unreasonable to expect them to wait for a very long time. It is incumbent on the person who wants to be shielded from spoilers to view things in a timely fashion. Just how long we must wait before some particular bit of information ceases to be a spoiler is complicated, and the rules associated with spoiling are different in different contexts and in different venues (for example, on fan pages, the prohibition on revealing certain bits of information is repealed fairly quickly—sometimes in just a matter of days, whereas in general conversation or on other forms of social media, the prohibition can remain in place for months or longer). We'll delve further into these issues in Chapter 10.

With these wrinkles in mind, we can amend our definition as follows:

(SP4): A spoiler is any information about a work of fiction (distinct from that work of fiction itself), including plays, novels, television programs, movies, etc., that has the potential to reveal

---

[9] Full disclosure: I'm not certain that there is an episode where Chuckles the Clown and Sue Ann Niven actually hook up. I seem to remember that there was. It's possible that I'm confabulating the episode where Sue Anne hooked up with Lou Grant. Initially, I was going to look this up, but soon realized that if it didn't actually happen, I don't want to know. It's just how I prefer to think of *The Mary Tyler Moore Show*.

some significant (or shocking) information that is neither common knowledge nor sufficiently old (as determined by context) to someone who has not yet encountered that information.

In subsequent chapters we will continue to make slight revisions to this definition, but this should be sufficient to give a fairly complete treatment of the philosophical issues pertaining to spoilers.

3
Things that Can Never Be Spoiled

The most recent modification to our definition of spoilers suggests that spoilers have a pretty short shelf life. While this is undoubtedly true in most cases, there is no shortage of counterexamples.

Suppose, for example, that I were to go up to a group of elementary school students and proclaim "Guess what, kids? Darth Vader is Luke Skywalker's father!"[1] Certainly there would be something wrong with my doing so, and that wrongness would be related to my spoiling what is perhaps the most significant part of the entire *Star Wars* saga. Clearly, I would be telling them a spoiler, even though it has been nearly forty years (as of the time this book is being prepared) since *The Empire Strikes Back* was released. Similarly, I can't tell the kids that Snape killed Dumbledore, nor can I tell them that the Planet of the Apes is Earth. In each case the spoiler shelf life has

---

[1] It's sort of fun to picture doing this by driving in front of an elementary school in the kind of car the Blues Brothers used to announce their big show. You know, a really old and beat up sedan with a giant industrial application speaker strapped to the top. "Attention all children! Come one, come all! Darth Vader was Luke Skywalker's Father!"

expired, but we judge that the information revealed counts as a legitimate spoiler. We need to reconcile the fact that these are spoilers with the fact that it does not jibe with the definition of spoilers that we have provided. There are a number of ways of doing this.

Reconciling Accounts

Perhaps the easiest and most intuitive way is to invoke the personal/impersonal spoiler distinction. We could maintain that the examples just given are not spoilers (in the impersonal sense) as the typical viewer standard yields the result that most people (or our hypothetical typical person) would not find the information significant or shocking (largely due to the fact that most typical fans have already seen or read *The Empire Strikes Back*, the *Harry Potter* series, and *Planet of the Apes*). Though they are spoilers in the personal sense. If we employ this strategy, then the prohibition against revealing this information is in place, since we ought not to reveal personal spoilers, and our definition of (impersonal) spoilers remains intact as well. It seems like a win-win solution.

There is, however, a pretty significant problem with this strategy. Recall that we are attempting to obtain a sort of reflective equilibrium between our theoretical account (the philosophical definition of spoilers that we settle on) and our pretheoretical intuitions (what ordinary, non-philosophical, users of the term "spoilers" are inclined to consider to be spoilers). Not only do ordinary speakers of English consider these to be instances of spoilers, most, if not all, consider them to be paradigmatic (standard or most widely accepted) instances.[2] So if we desire to have

---

[2] My evidence for this is largely anecdotal, but not insignificant. I've

an account of spoilers that lines up with the way folks use the word "spoiler" we need an account that treats these examples as full-on, legitimate spoilers (in the impersonal sense).

Let's consider a second strategy for reconciling our intuitive account of spoilers with our theoretical account. Note that it is relevant that there are a great many potential fans of each of these movies and books. While television shows such as *The Mary Tyler Moore Show* and movies such as *The Ghost and Mr. Chicken* may pick up a few more fans as time rolls on, *Star Wars*, *Harry Potter*, and *Planet of the Apes*, and their like promise to add legions to their list of faithful devotees. If part of the badness of spoilers is that they diminish the experience of the viewer (more on this in Chapter 7), then whether or not we should reveal the information under consideration is at least, in part, a function of whether or not doing so will lead to a diminished experience.

When we spoil something like *Star Wars* for a child, we are almost certainly diminishing a future viewing experience. The same for the *Harry Potter* series, *Planet of the Apes*, and scores of other shows. When we, however, spoil *The Mary Tyler Moore Show*, we are probably not diminishing a future experience, as the person who hears the spoiler is not likely going to ever view it, and even if they do view it someday, it is highly unlikely that they will have the sort of emotional attachment required for their experience to be diminished.

This provides us with a reason for treating the revealed information in the case of *Star Wars*, etc. as a true,

---

lectured on the philosophy of spoilers on numerous occasions, and nearly all participants in my discussions have agreed that the aforementioned examples are clearly spoilers.

spoiler, but not the revealed information in the case of the *Mary Tyler Moore Show*. This, of course, raises the question: why not just err on the side of caution, and never reveal any information that has the potential to diminish another's experience? The answer is that we don't want to do this since our desire not to diminish someone's experience needs to be balanced against other things we desire, such as our desire to discuss shows and movies that matter to us, as well as balanced against the responsibility that people have to view things, when possible, in a timely fashion, if they expect to be protected from hearing unwanted information.[3] So not only do we want to treat all cases like those under consideration as legitimate spoilers (spoilers in the impersonal sense), we want to do so in a way that respects a genuine desire not to reveal spoilers when it is inappropriate to do so, and holds no prohibition on the revealing of information when the prohibition is not warranted.

Notice that this can be accomplished by including potential fans in our typical viewer standard. In other words, we may want consider that the make-up of our typical viewer includes not only current fans, but future fans (including those fans who are not yet born). This has the effect of extending the shelf life of certain spoilers indefinitely (or at least until it no longer makes sense to include future fans of a particular work in the group of typical viewers). As long as there are generations to follow who will enjoy *Star Wars*, *Harry Potter*, and *Planet of the Apes*, reveals of significant information, on this view, will count as spoilers.

---

[3] I'm reminded of an episode of *The Simpsons* in which Homer, upon being caught in a lie, states "It takes two to lie. One to lie and one to listen." Avoiding spoilers is a two-way street. The "spoiler" needs to refrain from spoiling things, but the "spoilee" needs to position themselves to not have things spoiled.

There are a couple of worries, however, with this solution, as well. First, it's not obvious that future fans will find the same things significant (or even interesting). People tend to feel pretty strongly that the things that their generation loves will be loved equally (or at least to a great degree) by future generations. Sometimes this turns out to be true. Children dating back to the 1930s have loved the movie *The Wizard of Oz*. This, however, is far from the norm where appreciation of pop culture is concerned. For example, while kids today love pop music as much as ever, the pop music that they love is very different from the music that I listened to in my childhood. So, while my twelve-year-old self really loved bands such as Pink Floyd and artists such as Neil Young, my twelve-year-old son is more apt to listen to rap or hip-hop artists, such as Drake or Cardi B.[4] All of my peers back then assumed that everybody would love the music that we loved as much as we did (it seemed to us as if music had been perfected). A similar shift can be seen from the pop music my mother listened to in the 1950s (she was a big Sinatra fan) to the music I listened to in the 1970s. In fact, she was often surprised that I didn't have the exact same reaction to things that her generation felt was great.[5] While the changes in movie tastes haven't shifted quite as drastically during the same time period, there have been generational shifts in taste, and the same can be said for television, theater, and fiction. (I have a hard time picturing my

---

[4] On those occasions when I attempt to play some of my music for him, the most I can hope for is to be humored. Usually, I get an eye roll, and occasionally I detect some actual contempt for the music.

[5] I have fond memories of my mother forcing me to listen to her awful recordings by the Ray Conniff Singers while she gave me her "Am I right? Am I right?" look. I suspect that I didn't hide my contempt for her choices any better than my son hides his for mine.

son being excited to watch a show like *Bonanza*, except for perhaps its kitsch value.) The point is that an account of why some information should never be spoiled that is based on an expectation that there will be many future fans is doomed to fail, and likely sooner rather than later. Again, if what we're looking for is an account that captures the sentiment that some things should never be spoiled, a different rationale is required.

There is a second, perhaps deeper, problem with our current proposed solution: even were it not subject to the changing tastes objection, it seems to only apply to people of a certain age. This solution provides a reason not to spoil things for children, specifically, those who are too young to have had a reasonable chance to read or see the works under discussion here, but it doesn't apply to those who have had a chance, but have not yet done so. If we are going to reconcile our two accounts, we are going to need another solution; one that captures the intuition that certain things should never be spoiled (at least until someone gives their permission to spoil something).[6]

Related to this objection is the idea that our current proposed strategy seems to apply only to those whose cultures share certain features of their popular culture. For example, expanding the typical viewer standard to include future fans provides good reason to avoid telling *Star Wars* spoilers to folks in countries who are likely to see *Star Wars* at some point in the future, but, does not give us a good reason to avoid telling them to folks in countries who are not likely to see *Star Wars* at some point in the

---

[6] Even in cases in which permission is granted, good judgment should be exercised and discretion employed. Just as it would not be in my son's best interest to be told in advance what he is receiving for his birthday (no matter how much he wants to know), it's not always appropriate to reveal a spoiler to someone who asks you to tell them. Consider, for example, the case of someone who's watching a television series, has recorded the

future. So, if we maintain that certain spoilers should never be revealed, then this strategy will not do.[7]

A Great Solution

In taking stock we see that there are some things that purportedly should never be spoiled. In some cases, it is certain features of certain books, movies, plays, comic books, and television shows, such as a great plot twist or a surprise ending or, perhaps, a really great bit of dialogue, but in other cases it is virtually the entirety of those works that should never be spoiled. Many, for example, maintain that no one should reveal any facts about the *Harry Potter* books to those who have not yet read them, as each part is pure joy for the reader, whereas, it would be wrong to reveal the ending of *Avengers: Infinity War*, and some but not all plot points (again, with significance being the operative feature). Moreover, we need to reconcile the fact that some things should never be spoiled with the fact that spoilers tend to have a pretty short shelf life, and that we cannot reconcile these two things by appeal to the personal/impersonal spoiler distinction, nor can it be accomplished by appealing to the current popularity of

---

urrent episode, but "just can't wait" to find out the result of the cliff-hanger. I would not typically be inclined to give them the information they want. See Chapters 7 and 8 for further ideas on when it's inappropriate and when it's appropriate to spoil.

[7] Admittedly, I find myself on the fence on the issue of whether the prohibition against spoiling certain things extends universally. Were I to find myself in a remote part of the world, I'm not convinced that it would be terrible to describe the *Harry Potter* books in great detail. That said, in the interest of providing a philosophical treatment of spoilers that jibes with the norms of the relevant linguistic community (users of the term "spoiler"), we'll continue as if the universal prohibition is correct. I suspect that there are now just a very few places that have not heard of *Star Wars* or *Harry Potter*, anyway.

those things (by extending the current popularity to future fans).

Perhaps we can approach this from a different angle. What do the three examples we've been given have in common? In short, it is greatness. There is something great about *Star Wars, Harry Potter*, and *Planet of the Apes*. The idea is that we shouldn't spoil things that are great (whether the thing itself is great, as in the case of *Harry Potter* or some aspect of it is great, as in the case of the surprise ending of *Planet of the Apes*).[8]

This is a pretty straightforward idea, but one, I think, that comports nicely with our current practices. When people admonish others to not spoil that Snape killed Dumbledore or that the Planet of the Apes is Earth, it's precisely because they have a sort of reverence for that moment in the works (or for the entirety of the works). So, the solution is pretty simple: if something is great it should never be spoiled. Things can get a little tricky here. While it seems right to say that 1. no great work should be spoiled, and 2. no great part of an otherwise non-great work should be spoiled, there may be counterexamples to the second claim. These would be cases in which there was a great moment in a work that is otherwise truly unremarkable, which has already had its spoiler shelf life expire.

For example, consider a television show such as *Growing Pains*. This is a paradigmatic case of a thoroughly (at best) mediocre program. Suppose, that there existed one brilliant moment (perhaps a really fantastic twist or plot development) during one of the episodes. Our common-sense account of what can and cannot be spoiled would not consider that to be one of the things that can never be

---

[8] I actually think that *Planet of the Apes* is pretty great throughout, but am willing concede for the sake of argument that it is not on the same level as *The Empire Strikes Back* and the *Harry Potter* series.

spoiled. So, we can add to our account the caveat that, in the case of things that are great parts of otherwise not great works, that they must be part of a work that is, at minimum, held in pretty high esteem.

The greatness rationale for never spoiling certain things is virtuous in that it doesn't require that we invoke the personal/impersonal spoiler distinction, and it's not contingent on future viewers sharing the assessment of greatness. In fact, the greatness rationale doesn't even require a modification to our definition of spoilers. Since things that are great in the sense of the term being employed here can never be said to be *sufficiently* old, SP4 already entails that any information with the potential to reveal anything significant about them count as legitimate spoilers. So SP4 manages to carve out a special space for those things that are special without being at odds with our intuitive/common usage-based account.

What Is Greatness?

Thus far we haven't said much about what constitutes greatness, other than that we shouldn't spoil things that achieve greatness. There is good reason for this. Things can be great for a variety of reasons. A simple and pithy account of what constitutes greatness that contains any specifics will almost certainly exclude many things that are great (or future things that are both great and novel in their greatness). Conversely, a list of sufficient conditions for things exhibiting greatness would be unwieldly and cumbersome. Fortunately, one need not provide a foolproof philosophical definition of a concept, in order to pin down that concept (at least not for purposes such as ours). Thus, we can attempt to capture the notion of greatness by providing a few examples of the types of things that can be great.

Since we're concerned with both entire works that ought never to be spoiled and certain features of works that ought never to be spoiled, let's take up each separately. We'll start with the case of entire works that should never be spoiled, as it is the easier of the two.

The account of the greatness of these works that are considered too great to be spoiled will, of course, depend on the type of work that it is. There is no shortage of contentious philosophical literature on what makes for a great movie, or what makes for a great play, or what makes for a great comic book, and we don't need to settle the issue here. Suffice it to say that some shows and movies rise to a certain level of greatness, such that they should never be spoiled. Of course, the *Harry Potter* and *Star Wars* series fall into this category, as do the novels *Invisible Man*, and *Beloved*, just to give a handful of examples.[9]

Regarding features of works that should never be spoiled, we can be a little, but not much, more precise. First of all, we can limit the scope of what should never be spoiled (not what *is* a spoiler, as we've seen that many things can serve to spoil), to significant facts about the plot or the developments of the characters. These sorts of facts tend to include, but are not limited to, things such as, unexpected twists, details about who did it, surprise endings, the payoffs of story arcs, characters turning evil, characters turning good, whether a couple hooked up, specific bits of dialogue, and so forth.

Second, we can identify some of the things that make certain things significant. These things have to do with

---

[9] Sadly, a great number of novels fail to fall into the category of things that should never be spoiled because they're already spoiled. They are simply too "out there," so to speak. They are a part of our common knowledge. This list would include *The Great Gatsby*, the *Lord of the Rings* trilogy, *To Kill a Mockingbird*, and almost everything written by Faulkner, Tolstoy, Joyce, Dostoevsky, and Wilde (to name a few).

our cognitive, psychological, or emotional reactions to things. For example, those moments that leave our heads spinning, such as Snape killing Dumbledore, or those plot developments that cause us to spend hours thinking about the mechanics of them, or that cause us to reflect on why we didn't expect what we saw.

While these are important features, they don't tell us why certain things are so significant that they should never be spoiled. The contention here is, other than some hand-waving at it, it's not possible to give an account of what constitutes greatness with respect to significance. Again, things can be great for a whole host of reasons.

This raises an important issue. If there exists no clearly defined set of criteria for determining greatness, how does one know what's great? Perhaps it's just the sort of thing we can recognize a good percentage of the time. Given that most folks don't agree too terribly much on what counts as great, this is probably not the most reliable method (this entails that most people will be wrong most of the time). Since few, if any, of us are infallible distinguishers of greatness from non-greatness, we're just going to have to hedge our bets somewhat. Here I think the community can be a great resource. If we consider those things that it is generally agreed upon that one should never spoil, then we will likely be able to avoid spoiling things that, in actuality, should never be spoiled.

Is this guaranteed to get the right result? Absolutely not. Is that bad for our view? Absolutely not. Our view is not committed to the position that we can know which things are great (and hence should never be spoiled). It's only committed to the view that great things should never be spoiled. Our inability to always know what is great is just a feature of human knowledge—it's our epistemic predicament, so to speak. Our view can be seen as analogous to those moral theories, such as utilitarianism, that maintain that we should always bring about the best state of affairs, while acknowledging, given our limited epistemic vantage points, that we may not always be able to know what the best state of affairs is (or which of our actions will lead to the best state of affairs). Yet, according to those views, if you bring about the best state of affairs you've done the right thing, and if you don't you haven't. Similarly, if you spoil something great, then you have done something wrong.

Since thinking something is great, doesn't make it great (even if everyone or almost everyone thinks it is great), the hive-mind is not guaranteed to get things right one hundred percent of the time, but, as I said, they appear to be right more often than not. Alongside the examples we've been considering in this chapter we find perched atop the Mount Olympus of spoilers that Norman Bates is "Mother," Dorothy's trip to Oz was all a dream, every suspect on the Orient Express took part in the killing, Soylent Green is people, and *To Serve Man* is a cookbook. See Appendix 1 for a more comprehensive list of the greatest spoilers of all time.

One famous example of something that is generally considered to be a thing that should never be spoiled, is the payoff of the movie *Citizen Kane*, namely, that Kane's dying word "Rosebud" refers to his childhood sled. When I lecture on spoilers, this almost always comes up as an example on the never spoil list. To be honest, it's not clear to me why it's thought to be significant in the relevant sense. To be sure, it's part of the statement that the film is making (that great wealth and power don't guarantee happiness), but the film makes that statement quite well without finding out that his inexpensive sled was the source of his greatest happiness. Really, Kane's uttering "Rosebud" was more of a MacGuffin—a plot device to motivate characters' actions, which is otherwise pretty insignificant. Had the movie started by telling us that Rosebud brought Kane more joy than anything else, and then continued in pretty much the same way as it did, it would be every bit as good. So, the community sometimes get things wrong, but it's probably the best guide we've got.

4
What Else Can Be Spoiled?

Recall that our current definition of a spoiler is SP4:

(SP4): A spoiler is any information about a work of fiction (distinct from that work of fiction itself), including plays, novels, television programs, movies, that has the potential to reveal some significant (or shocking) information that is neither common knowledge nor sufficiently old (as determined by context) to someone who has not yet encountered that information.

Notice that SP4 restricts spoilers to works of fiction. On the face of things, there are a couple of good reasons for doing so. First, it comports nicely with how we normally use the term "spoiler," and getting our theoretical account to jibe with our common usage of the term "spoiler" is one of our primary goals in this section. Second, many things that are not fiction are things that it is not wrong to spoil. For example, people tend to want to know the news right away. There is no prohibition against informing people of things occurring in the world, as doing so prior to their getting that information from, say, a more institutional source, doesn't harm them (for example, by diminishing their experience) in the way that spoiling something does.

Often, having more information has the opposite effect—
it benefits people (knowledge is power, kids!).

So, it's clear that you cannot spoil the news. But what
about things that 1. aren't fiction, 2. are things people may
not want to know about as soon as possible, and 3. are
things such that revealing significant information about
them is not obviously beneficial to the persons given the
information (in fact, may be detrimental)? Are there such
things, and can they be legitimately spoiled? Let's consider the question of whether our current definition of a
spoiler should be expanded to include some things that
are not works of fiction.

A Devil of a Case

SP4, as was mentioned in Chapter 2, is mostly right in
that it captures most instances of our ordinary usage of
the term "spoiler." Suppose, however, that just as you were
sitting down to read Erik Larson's book *The Devil in the
White City* a passerby says "It's really fun when H.H.
Holmes is finally arrested. They catch him in Philadelphia
on an insurance fraud charge." According to our definition
that would not count as a spoiler (since *The Devil in the
White City* is not a work of fiction), and yet, it would feel
as if it were spoiled. Part of the reading experience would
be diminished, and plenty of the suspense of earlier parts
of the story would dissipate. It sure seems like a spoiler.
Moreover, most people would call it a spoiler (even if most
of the time when we are using the term "spoiler" we are
referring to fiction). Especially given that Erik Larson
writes nonfiction in a novelistic style.

So how does this case differ from the nonfiction cases
discussed in Chapter 2? There we talked about historical
events as common knowledge. By and large, people will
watch television shows, such as *The Tudors,* to see (among

other things) the story of Anne Boleyn's beheading unfold. They will watch *Vesuvius* to see the volcano's eruption as a backdrop for an otherwise fictional story.[1] It's the fact of their being common knowledge that is part of the draw. Conversely, with what we can call "fictionesque nonfiction," such as *The Devil in the White City*, most readers know only a little bit about the topic, and most of the content, while all being true, plays much like fiction.[2] The right thing to conclude is that as long as nonfiction is being presented as entertainment in this way (that is, as something that is designed to bring about reactions similar to those we experience when we encounter works of fiction), we can and should include it in the category of things that can be legitimately spoiled.

In light of this, we can modify our working definition to incorporate fictionesque nonfiction as follows:

(SP5): A spoiler is any information about a work of entertainment (distinct from that work of entertainment itself), including plays, novels, television programs, and movies, that has the potential to reveal some significant (or shocking) information that is neither common knowledge nor sufficiently old (as determined by context) to someone who has not yet encountered that information.[3]

---

[1] To be honest, I don't actually know why anyone wanted to see *Vesuvius*.

[2] I'm using the expression "fictionesque nonfiction" to capture what Larson and others are doing, namely, presenting nonfiction in the style of fiction. This is not to be confused with historical fiction, such as Victor Hugo's *The Hunchback of Notre Dame*, which uses historical events as a backdrop to a fictional (or mostly fictional) story. Regarding spoilers, historical fiction can just be lumped in with other fiction, as all the same considerations apply (common knowledge cannot be spoiled, significant other plot points can, and so on).

[3] One might argue that the news counts as entertainment, and hence satisfies our current definition (SP5). I take it that while the news has entertainment value, and over the years there have been efforts to make it

Other Cases of Nonfiction

One upshot to this point is that some instances of nonfiction, for example, fictionesque nonfiction, can be spoiled. This raises the question of whether there are other instances of nonfiction than can be legitimately spoiled.

We've already seen that news stories (at least generally speaking) cannot be spoiled.[4] What about sporting events? Can things that occur in a sporting event be spoiled? Undoubtedly! Sporting events have much in common with works of fiction. In virtue of there being winners and losers and other forms of competition, there are story arcs. Furthermore, there are backstories of human interest (such as people overcoming adversity, injures, or their fears), there is interpersonal drama ("These coaches have despised one another since they were opponents in the championship game back in 1997"), there are other forms of drama (such as, who will win?), we find ourselves emotionally invested in sporting events, and so on. Moreover, there are plenty of significant things about sporting events that might get revealed: who won, who scored, who was injured, whether the game was dramatic or a snoozer, and whether a particular player broke a particular record (to give just a handful of examples).

Our reactions to having information about sporting events revealed can also bear a strong resemblance to our reactions to having other spoiler information revealed. On a number of occasions I've gone to great lengths to ensure that I don't learn the results of a ballgame that I'm recording for later in the day: I don't look at any news sources (I

---

more entertaining [insert diatribe about the short attention spans of most people], it still should not be individuated as a work of entertainment. Its primary purpose is to be informative.

  [4] This claim gets qualified a bit because every now and then the news will give information about entertainment that qualifies as a spoiler.

avoid television, the Internet, turn off notifications on my phone), I notify friends and co-workers that I'm recording a game, and so forth, only to have the game spoiled by someone I couldn't have reasonably foreseen would have spoiled it for me. On one particular occasion I had a flight during an NFL playoff game. My favorite team (the San Francisco 49ers!) were playing, so I had a strong rooting interest. I had set-up my DVR one week in advance. I had managed to avoid hearing any conversations about the game or looking at any televisions while in the airport. I figured that as long as I plugged in my headphones, I wouldn't hear anyone talking about the game on the plane. Suddenly, the pilot came on the intercom and announced the results. The announcement actually came through the headphones I was using to avoid hearing the score.[5] I was furious! Not only was I denied the experience of seeing the game (at least with all the excitement that comes with not knowing the result), I was not given a chance of not hearing the result. I'm not alone in this. It's not uncommon for sports fans to go to great lengths to avoid hearing things about matches that they will not be watching until later, and when sports are spoiled for them they become quite upset.

Taking stock, we see that sporting events contain all the essential elements required to be spoilable that other forms of entertainment have: they have all the elements of good narrative, they contain significant information, which can potentially be revealed, and they tend to engender the same sorts of reactions to receiving information

---

[5] This isn't the only time this happened to me. On another occasion I boarded a plane with the intention of watching Game Six of the 2002 World Series once I arrived home. Again, my favorite baseball team, the San Francisco Giants, were playing the Anaheim Angels. I had done a pretty good job of avoiding the results when the pilot announced the scores. This time, I half expected it.

when one has attempted to avoid the information. Furthermore, increasingly, people have employed the language of spoilers in sports contexts. If a pilot were to announce a sporting result over the intercom today, they would likely be met with cries of "Spoiler alert!" Given that sporting events being spoilable is consistent with both our current definition (SP5) and our ordinary language use of the term "spoiler," the right thing to conclude is that sports can also be spoiled.

One difference between sports and the other forms of entertainment that we consider spoilable, is that there's a stronger expectation that we will not spoil books, plays, or movies. If I want to ensure that no one will tell me the results of a ballgame, I usually have to inform people that I've not yet seen it, I'll be watching it later, that I'm recording it, I don't currently know the results, and that I don't want to know the results. So, with sports—somewhat like with the news—the expectation is that you don't object to receiving information, unless you have made it explicit that you don't want it. With, movies and other works of fiction, the expectation is that you don't reveal spoilers, until you confirm that the person you're speaking to is ready to discuss it.[6] This difference, does not, however, provide a reason for thinking that we shouldn't consider sports spoilers to be legitimate spoilers; rather, it just

---

[6] If you're not feeling the force of this consider how you think people in the following scenarios would react. Scenario 1: The Chicago Cubs have just won an important game. The game was played in the afternoon. A guy sitting at his desk at work upon completion of the game stands up in his cubicle and shouts for all to hear "Cubs, Baby!" Most likely there would not be any objections raised. Or possibly someone who had recorded the game would calmly say "Darn, I was going to watch it later." Scenario 2: Same guy plays hooky from work and goes to the movies. He shows up just before quitting time and exclaims "Whoa, Thanos killed Spiderman!" In this scenario I think people would be furious, and they wouldn't be shy about letting him know it.

demonstrates that the social norms of sports spoilers are not as far along in their development (perhaps they're akin to the etiquette surrounding movie and television spoilers twenty or thirty years ago).

The above considerations would appear to apply equally to other forms of entertainment that share the same essential elements with works of fiction, as does sports. This would include other forms of competition (such as the National Spelling Bee), certain reality television shows (such as *Survivor*), certain documentaries (for instance *Hoop Dreams*), certain awards programs (such as *The Academy Awards*), and certain game shows (for example *Jeopardy*).

Between Fiction and Nonfiction

We've now expanded our account of legitimate spoilers to include many instances of fiction and a number of instances of nonfiction. It appears that if we've been sufficiently thorough, then we should be ready to move on to the next topic, as the literal interpretation of "nonfiction" would include anything that is not fiction. The literal interpretation, however, does capture the customary sense of the word, so appearances, in this case, are deceiving. Typically, "nonfiction" refers to a work that is mostly or completely based in fact, as opposed to being made up, and hence is not just anything that isn't fiction. This raises the question of whether there is anything that doesn't fall neatly into either category (fiction or nonfiction) that can be spoiled. More specifically, this raises the question of whether things that are non-narrative art forms, such as visual forms of art or instrumental music, can be spoiled.

We could easily imagine that upon hearing detailed information about a new jazz number by Keith Jarrett or about a new sculpture by artist Damien Hirst prior to having experienced the works for themselves some people might be annoyed in the same way that you get annoyed upon hearing an unwanted spoiler. In fact, under such circumstances you might even say "Spoiler alert!" or admonish the person who revealed the information for spoiling it. In such cases, however, we're talking about personal spoilers, and not legitimate spoilers. This is because, while containing information that some folks may not want revealed, generally information of this sort is not considered significant using our typical viewer standard.[7] Most fans of music and visual arts just don't care that much, were they to find out that a new composition is in a minor key, or a new album is mostly instrumental, or that a new sculpture has an even bigger shark in formaldehyde, and so on.

Are Trailers Spoilers?

This pretty much completes our treatment of the sorts of things that can be spoiled. Before moving on, however, let's consider one additional question. Are trailers spoilers?

The short answer is that they can be, but they need not be. To the extent that they reveal information about movies or television shows that is significant to people who haven't yet encountered that information, they are spoilers. Not every trailer is a spoiler, as some trailers don't provide much by way of significant information, but most trailers are chock full of it.

---

[7] While this is generally the case there may be some exceptions, which rise to the level of legitimate spoilers. Rachel Robison-Greene suggests the following examples. Suppose that you go to a modern art exhibit and find yourself sitting in a chair only to realize that, much to your surprise, the fact of your sitting in the chair is part of the exhibit—you've become part of the art. Such an experience could certainly be spoiled. Similarly, suppose that you come across a link on social media that ultimately leads to the rickrolling of the person who clicks on the link. Revealing that in advance to someone would constitute a spoiler (although you would be doing them a solid by spoiling that particular experience).

If trailers are spoilers, are the people who make and distribute trailers (the movie companies) and the people who show trailers (the movie house owners) doing something wrong? Here are a few reasons for thinking that they are not doing anything wrong most of the time. First, people who go to the movies (and people who watch television programs on commercial television) are aware that the trailers will be shown. Most people actually seem to like the trailers (or at least they don't mind them too much). So, they are being shown in a context in which it is expected that the spoilers will be given.[8]

Second, it's not hard to avoid trailers. You can wait until the trailers have ended before entering the movie house.[9] Third, having to sit though trailers has become part of the cost of seeing the kinds of movies that are being made today. Given that movies cost millions of dollars to make, they will not generally be profitable unless lots of people go to see them. Trailers are great advertising, and get people to watch new films. So, there is an unwritten contract between the movie industry and movie goers: fans endure the advertising in the form of trailers, and the movie companies keep making the massively expensive films. Given that the context is one where everyone knows what's contained in trailers (even if everyone doesn't consider them to be instances of spoilers) and everyone knows that a number of trailers will definitely be shown prior to the feature presentation, the showing of trailers before a movie begins can be seen as

---

[8] This is not always a mitigating factor. For example, a person at work who always reveals spoilers doesn't get off the hook just because folks come to expect it.

[9] I can't speak for theaters everywhere, but the ones in my community all show trailers for almost exactly twenty minutes. It's easy to avoid the trailers, and time one's entrance to a movie. I try to arrive at my seat during either the Coca-Cola commercial or the Dolby Digital Sound commercial.

being analogous to a case where someone gives a spoiler alert sufficiently far in advance of revealing the spoiling information as to allow folks to avoid hearing that information. The badness of spoiling does not obtain in these cases.

That said, just as not all spoilers are created equal, not all trailers are created equal. It is reasonable to expect to see some significant information about an upcoming movie in a trailer, as we said, it is part of the cost of doing business, so to speak. "Some" is the operative word. What we have come to expect over time is to hear a few of the jokes, perhaps a tag line or two, and get an idea of some of the major narrative points (who the protagonist is, who the antagonist is, what's the main issue, what type of film it is, and so on). We have also come to expect a little misdirection from time to time. Occasionally a trailer will make it look like you are getting one kind of movie, perhaps a horror film, when, in fact, the film is a different kind of movie altogether, maybe a comedy. If the misdirection isn't too misleading, it's actually a good thing. It reduces the amount that the trailer actually spoils the film, and the mere existence of some trailers misdirecting casts a nice bit of doubt on the veracity of many other trailers. It's as if misdirection paints a big "maybe!" on much of what one sees in trailers.

Still, there is a recent phenomenon that seems to thumb its nose at these norms and conventions. More and more we are getting trailers that contain so much information, that we know virtually the entirety of the plot (perhaps except the predictable "couple winds up together after all" ending). A "good" example of this is the trailer for *Mission Impossible: Fallout*.[10] When we go to the

---

[10] To be honest, I didn't mind it on this occasion. The trailer for *Mission Impossible: Fallout* did a nice job of reassuring me that I would not enjoy seeing this movie under any circumstances whatsoever.

movies, we expect to see trailers, but we don't expect to have entire films spoiled or have nearly all the funny parts of a comedy shown.[11] It's not obvious why the film companies do this. It seems that there are at least as many people who become disinclined to pay to see a film in which they pretty much know all the twists, turns, and funny bits, as there are people who, upon viewing one of these "whole plot" trailers decide to see the film. Given that the spoilers revealed under these circumstances exceed what people reasonably expect to see, the tacit spoiler alert described previously, doesn't apply. Under circumstances such as these, the folks who show trailers that disclose the entire plot or reveal most of the funny parts, are doing something morally wrong. This phenomenon, by the way, is no longer restricted to movie trailers. HBO and Showtime have begun putting way too much information in their promotional materials. A case in point is HBO's trailer for Season Two of *The Deuce*. Upon seeing this I felt that I already knew about fifty percent of the story arcs and at least twenty-five percent of the unexpected twists.[12]

---

[11] A related, but equally annoying, recent trend is when the trailer for a horror film shows the slasher, villain, or monster. Horror movies very frequently create suspense by not revealing what the villain looks like, and then presenting it to the viewers at just the right moment. In fact, some films never give you a complete look at the baddie. When the really scary thing appears in the trailer, then that suspense is wasted.

[12] In a particularly annoying variation on this theme, the producers of *American Horror Story* released photographs of all the characters each of their featured actors would be playing (often on *American Horror Story* certain actors play multiple roles) just prior to the first episode of Season Eight: *Apocalypse*. One of the really fun facts about *Apocalypse* is that it was teased that certain characters from Season One: *Murder House* and Season Three: *Coven* would make appearances, but they didn't tell which characters. This promo did that. Ugh!

5
Vagueness and Spoilers

Vagueness raises a number of issues pertaining to spoilers, some of which are quite controversial. For instance, a number of people seem to think that we can avoid spoiling something merely by being vague. The idea is that as long as a specific plot point is not being revealed, then nothing is being spoiled. As we learned in Chapter 2, spoilers are not just limited to plot points (again, consider a case where someone spoils something by revealing information about where filming is occurring, and makes it easy for folks to deduce specific plot developments). So, can we avoid spoiling by being vague? Are vague spoilers an acceptable form of spoiling? How vague is "vague enough" when it comes to spoiling something?

Getting Clear about Vague Spoilers

The term "vague" has multiple senses. For instance, it can mean "admitting of borderline cases." Borderline cases are cases where it is not exactly clear whether a particular term applies. For example, the word "tall" is somewhat vague in that it clearly applies to men who are over seven feet tall, clearly does not apply to men who are under five feet tall, and it is not clear whether it applies to men who are precisely six feet tall.[1] Some would say it does apply and others would say that it does not.

Another sense of the term "vague" is "lacking a certain, clear, or definite meaning." For example, if I were to assert that "there was drama at the funeral" my lack of specificity regarding the drama would count as an instance of vagueness. Similarly, if when queried about where I am heading and I say something general such as "out" or "to a store," my response would count as vague (in this second sense). Vagueness in the first sense, does not pose any special problems for our account of spoilers, but vagueness in the second sense does, as does the related concept: ambiguity. For convenience sake, we will treat ambiguity as a particular kind of vagueness.[2]

The week that *Avengers: Infinity War* was released, social media was chock full of vague statements about the movie. They ranged greatly in detail and specificity. One person posted on Facebook "O.M.G.!!!!! The first ten minutes!" Another wrote "You won't believe who died." Another wrote, "There had better be a sequel to bring them all back to life." These are just a few examples. I literally saw about thirty or so posts such as these in the week after the release date. In each case, each post contained a number of comments that admonished the original poster to not spoil.[3] Are these spoilers? To the extent that they

---

[1] Context is important in cases such as these. For example, if we're talking about professional basketball players, then 6' tall would likely count as short, and the relevant borderline cases pertain to people who are around 6' 5" tall.

[2] Ambiguous terms and ambiguous expressions don't lack specificity. Their meaning is determinate. The problem is that more than one possible determinate meaning presents itself. "He is old" is vague. "He saw him in his car" is ambiguous.

[3] There were many other things said to the original posters, but

meet our current definition, in particular (I'd hate to be vague here), to the extent that they potentially reveal something significant, indeed, they are spoilers. Prior to seeing the film, I was able to deduce from these and other postings that a major character died in the first ten minutes and that a number of other major characters died. Moreover, it was clear that some of the major characters that died were Marvel Cinematic Universe superheroes.[4]

How Vague Is Too Vague?

Certainly not every vague statement about a work of entertainment will count as a spoiler, even if it is about a new release, etc. For example, if upon leaving *Ocean's 8* I exclaim to those purchasing tickets for the next showing that "something significant happened," the lack of detail, that is, the degree of vagueness, in my statement prevents it from being a spoiler (even though my utterance pertains to something significant about the movie). Were I to

---

common decency prevents me from rehearsing them here. Suffice to say that things got pretty ugly that week on the old interwebs.

[4] Some of the aforementioned spoilers were sufficient to spoil things by themselves. Others did not quite rise to the level of stand-alone spoilers, but in combination with other things that were posted, provided enough information to spoil something significant. This means that it is possible for someone to be part of a spoiling without actually revealing a spoiler. So, when considering whether to post something, we should not just consider whether what we are posting is, in fact, a spoiler, but also whether what we are posting can lead to something being spoiled for someone. For that matter, we should consider whether what we are saying might lead to a spoiler being revealed, even if what we are saying is sufficiently vague as to not constitute a spoiler on its own. Greg Spendlove proposes the following sort of case. Suppose that I say something so vague as to not constitute a legitimate spoiler, but it leads someone else to clarify by filling in the details. In such a case my non-spoiler is an essential part of the causal chain that led to a spoiling. Under such circumstances, it would have been better for me not to have uttered the vague statement.

exclaim instead (about the same event) that "there was a twist during the heist" I still wouldn't be spoiling anything, as 1. the twist during the heist is a staple of Soderbergh's *Ocean's* franchise that audiences have come to expect, and 2. while containing much more detail than my first utterance, my exclamation still fails to provide enough detail to count as potentially revealing something significant about the movie. Suppose, instead, I were to exclaim that "there's a twist during the heist that involves the mark actually being in on the heist, but the others did not know it." This would clearly be a spoiler. If you had that information prior to seeing the film, it would adversely affect your viewing experience, as that information comes as a huge reveal towards the end of the film—the surprise would be ruined. Still, my statement is somewhat vague. It doesn't make the twist explicit (that the heist was actually two separate heists occurring simultaneously).

There are two things of note to glean from these cases. First, vagueness admits of degrees. One statement can be more or less vague than another. Second, there is a threshold that a vague statement crosses when it becomes a spoiler. Of course, that threshold may be different for different statements depending on a variety of factors, such as the type of work the statement is about (knowing that the protagonist uses a weapon in a movie may be a big reveal if the movie is a rom-com, but not so much if the movie is a western), the amount of background information about the work that is common knowledge (for example, fans tend to know quite a bit about particular franchises), and whether particular information about the actors and directors involved in the work has the potential to reveal significant plot information (for example, knowing that there are explosions in a movie may be a reveal if one doesn't know much about the actors or the director, but not if one knows that Michael Bay directed the film in which it occurs), just to identify a few factors.

Sometimes the mere mention of spoilers can be a spoiler. Mark Hamill's admonition to fans to not reveal spoilers for *Star Wars: The Force Awakens* led fans to rightly conclude that there was a twist. Moreover, some savvy fans were even able to deduce the twist, namely that Han Solo dies in the film. It was a "methinks thou dost protest too much" moment, and it drew real attention to the possibility of an unexpected plot twist.

Another interesting kind of vague spoiler is the non-verbal spoiler. This occurs when someone makes a gesture or has a facial expression that reveals something significant about a work of art. Suppose for example, that upon exiting a movie such as *The Fault in Our Stars* I make a "tear drop falling" gesture to those waiting to enter the theater.[5] My doing so would likely signal to the movie-goers that one of the main characters died in the end. This would count as a legitimate spoiler. Of course, a more vague gesture (for example, a facial expression that indicated that the film was intense) would not cross the threshold into the category of legitimate spoilers.

There is an interesting class of vague statements about the sort of works we have been considering (potentially spoilable works) that involve saying something about the work, but not in a way that either reveals significant plot details or would allow anyone to deduce a significant plot detail, nor do they reveal something particularly shocking. These would involve statements such as *"Jurassic World: Fallen Kingdom* really sucked," *"Black Panther* is fantastic; maybe the best of the Marvel Cinematic Universe."

---

[5] In the interest of full disclosure: I had to Google the plot to this one. To put this in the language of contemporary metaphysicians there are no close possible worlds in which I could be compelled to see this film. Ugh!

"The pacing of *A Quiet Place* was really slow, but done in a way that created wonderful suspense," and "The new Woody Allen movie is an homage to Fellini."[6]

What I find interesting about these examples and others of the same general variety is that 1. they are clearly not spoilers, as they don't satisfy our definition of a spoiler, 2. almost no one thinks that they are spoilers, so treating them as non-spoilers is consistent with our goal of having our account of what constitutes a spoiler jibe with the ordinary usage of the term "spoiler," but 3. oddly enough, people will often react to hearing such things in the same way that they react to spoilers—generally speaking, most people just don't want to be told such things. There is a good reason for this. Just as people don't want to have works of art spoiled for them, they also resist having their expectations for what they are about to read or view, affected in advance.

For example, virtually everyone has had the experience at one time or another of not enjoying a film or a television program or a book as much as they thought they were going to, because of the degree to which it had been hyped up by their friends and family members.[7] For me, the most noteworthy example of this was *Fight Club*.[8] To be sure, I

---

[6] I didn't cite an actual example for this one as 1. I stopped watching Woody Allen films a long time ago (way before the allegations against him were levied, around the time his movies stopped being funny and became even more pretentious than they had been), and 2. all his films strike me as being homages to Fellini (except his occasional homage to German expressionism), so I'm pretty sure the example will ring true as given.

[7] Sometimes the opposite will happen, where lots of folks will downplay something so much that upon watching it you will be pleasantly surprised, but that seems to happen with less frequency than the converse.

[8] Some other instances of this general phenomenon include: almost anything by Ernest Hemingway (except for *The Sun Also Rises*), *Citizen Kane* (which I think is great, but not *that* great), *Forrest Gump*, *Gladiator*, and the television shows *Cheers* and *Oz*.

enjoyed it a lot, but still managed to leave the theater somewhat disappointed, because I was expecting to love it more than I did. So, having little or no expectations for something in advance (or for having only one's own expectations) is usually considered to be a good thing (and in those cases where it's not, such as cases where someone is on the fence about watching or reading something, people can seek out recommendations). It's not just our expectations of the quality of a work of art that we don't want to have affected. We don't, generally speaking, want to know anything about what we can come to expect from a work other than very general things such as the type of work that it is (for instance "It's a work of science fiction!") or who it features ("It stars Paul Rudd!").

A New Non-Spoiler Kind of Spoiler

Part of the reason that spoilers have become such an issue is that people love to spoil things. They don't necessarily want the bad consequences that come with spoiling something, meaning that they don't want to actually ruin or diminish someone else's experience; rather, they want to tell people about things they've viewed or read, and they want to do it first.[9] People just can't keep a secret, and that's essentially what spoilers are. This is why some folks (I'm looking at you, my dear sister) are dying to tell you what gift they got you before you have the opportunity to open it.[10] A very recent phenomenon has emerged that allows folks to reveal spoilers, but in a way that is so vague and

---

[9] This is not to say that no one wants to ruin other people's viewing experience, there are plenty of jerks out there, but most spoilers occur because people have a hard time holding on to interesting information.

[10] In fairness to my sister, she hasn't done this in about ten years, which coincidentally, is when we started giving one another gift cards when presents are exchanged.

cryptic that nothing actually ever gets spoiled. These reveals are called "spoilers without context."

It's not clear where spoilers without context got their start, but they came to prominence just after the release of *Avengers: Infinity War*.[11] Fans who wanted to share something, perhaps anything, about the movie, but didn't want to ruin the experience of others (or at minimum didn't want to get taken to task for spoiling or be labelled a "spoiler") began posting cryptic pictures on social media (mostly on Twitter at first) of things tangentially related to key moments in the film, but in such a way that no one could possibly deduce what the picture was in reference to. For example, at various times in *Avengers: Infinity War* Thor refers to Rocket Racoon as a rabbit. On Twitter a bunch of people just tweeted pictures of a rabbit. Others posted pictures of piles of dirt, in reference to Thanos turning half the population of the universe to something like dust or ash. Perhaps the most ubiquitous of the spoilers without context were various pictures of Squidward (from *Spongebob Squarepants*).[12] Tony Stark referred to Ebony Maw as Squidward.

The exceedingly vague nature of spoilers without context prevents them from being spoilers at all, but there is something ingenious behind them. Once you've seen the movie, you're in position to appreciate the spoilers. It's sort of like having a puzzle to solve ("How did that picture of a rabbit connect with the movie?), but one that doesn't have an adverse effect on the viewer. In fact, it often en-

---

[11] <http://www.thisisinsider.com/avengers-infinity-war-spoilers-without-context-2018-4>.

[12] It didn't stop there. Once the Squidward posts went viral, there was a short-lived but popular Twitter movement that involved telling all the *Avengers: Infinity War* spoilers without context possible using only *Spongebob Squarepants* memes.

hances the experience. Think of it as a win-win for both the person who posts the spoiler without context and for the person who views the post.

Are Vague Spoilers Okay?

As was mentioned at the onset of this chapter, just after *Avengers: Infinity War* was released the Internet was loaded with spoilers. Many of these spoilers were vague, but still managed to spoil important plot points. It's not controversial whether vague spoilers are legitimate spoilers (again, provided that they've crossed the threshold into meeting our definition of a spoiler). It is somewhat controversial whether it's acceptable to give vague spoilers.

While there is generally much agreement over whether the revealing of some particular bit of information is a spoiler and nearly as much agreement over the badness of spoiling (people generally agree that we should not reveal spoilers), there is some real disagreement over whether it is bad to reveal vague spoilers (even if they rise to the level of legitimate spoiler). Many of the admonitions on social media to not spoil around the time of the release of *Avengers: Infinity War* were met with the response that vague spoilers are okay. So, comments such as "O.M.G.!!!!! The first ten minutes!" "You won't believe who died" and "There had better be a sequel to bring them all back to life" are considered by some to be spoilers, but ones that it is acceptable to reveal in virtue of their vagueness. One upshot of there not being a consensus regarding vague spoilers (that is, of some people feeling that there is no prohibition on vague spoilers and others feeling that there is one), is that it makes it impossible for our theoretical account of the badness of spoilers to achieve the same sort of equilibrium with the lay view of the badness of spoilers as we find with our account of what constitutes a spoiler.

Recall that our theoretical account of what constitutes a spoiler jibes nicely with the way the term "spoiler" is commonly used by lay persons.

We will discuss the badness of spoiling in further detail in Chapters 6 and 7, but at minimum we should point out that to the extent that vague spoilers have the same potential to reveal something significant about a work of art as non-vague spoilers, and to the extent that revealing something significant potentially has an adverse effect on our experiencing of that work, there is no reason to think that the prohibition against vague spoilers should be any different from the prohibition against non-vague spoilers. Moreover, we don't encounter arguments for the view that vague spoilers are okay. It tends to just get asserted.

While we certainly see more backlash against vague spoilers than we find support for them, those who hold the view that vague spoilers are acceptable are not a small and isolated group. There are a couple of reasons for this. First, the aforementioned desire to discuss current programs, movies, and books is strong. People are compelled to discuss works of art that move them. Recall that this led some to provide spoilers without context. Those who reveal vague spoilers are just going a little farther. This in combination with the fact that people tend to assess the morality of their own actions in self-interested ways, leads those who are compelled to give vague spoilers, to interpret their doing so, as morally permissible.[13] Second, there is a somewhat recent phenomenon that subtly reinforces the notion that vague spoilers are in a different moral category from non-vague spoilers: the vague spoiler warning. "Vague Spoiler Warning" is now a popular hashtag. The idea be-

---

[13] For a nice discussion of this phenomenon see <https://www.scientificamerican.com/article/most-people-consider-themselves-to-be-morally-superior>.

hind the vague spoiler warning is a good one. It is a form of spoiler warning, so someone who doesn't want to encounter any spoilers will heed its warning just as they would a regular spoiler warning, but those who only want to avoid highly specific spoilers can choose to ignore it.

There are a couple of problems, however, with vague spoiler warnings. First implicit in them is the idea that if a spoiler is vague, then it must not spoil anything terribly significant. As we've seen, this is just not true. Suppose that I tell someone who is about to see *The Empire Strikes Back* that Luke is related to one of the other major characters. Even though I'm being vague, by not saying that it is Darth Vader, I'm still revealing more than I ought to reveal. Vague spoilers can be very significant. Second, as mentioned, the existence of vague spoiler warnings reinforces the idea that revealing vague spoilers is not as bad as revealing non-vague spoilers. Since they serve a good purpose, it is incumbent on people to understand that vague spoilers can be just as significant and the revealing of vague spoilers can be just as bad as is the case with non-vague spoilers.

II

The Ethics of
Spoilers

6
Is It Bad to Spoil?

Thus far our desire to have our theoretical account of spoilers comport nicely with our pretheoretical intuitions is going well. Our account has an independent theoretical basis, and it doesn't run afoul of what most non-philosophers are inclined to consider legitimate spoilers, nor does it deviate from how we tend to speak about spoilers. So far so good.

People, as we've seen, tend to get pretty upset when they've had something spoiled for them (some people even resort to stabbing in the chest those who reveal spoilers!). But what if our more reasonable reactions to spoilers are not warranted? What if spoilers are not bad at all? It's not uncommon for people to react negatively to things that are actually beneficial for them. Consider a case of a child who gets terribly upset upon learning that she is on the way to a dental appointment. Similarly, consider a case where political rhetoric convinces people to vote for policies that will ultimately harm them. It is at least possible that we get worked up about spoilers, even though there is nothing bad about having something spoiled. This possibility, if correct, would have pretty severe consequences for our account of spoilers.

When Social Scientists Spoil Spoilers

As mentioned in our brief history of spoilers, in 2011 a pair of researchers from University of California, San Diego—Jonathan D. Leavitt and Nicholas J.S. Christenfeld—released the results of a study which concluded that people actually had a slight but significant preference for spoiled stories over unspoiled stories. The title of their paper nicely summarizes their conclusion: "Story Spoilers Don't Spoil Stories."[1]

Here's how the study was conducted. There were 819 subjects. Each subject read three different types of short stories: an ironic twist story, a mystery, and an evocative literary story. Spoilers were prepared for each story that revealed its ending. (Note that this study is restricted to ending spoilers only, and would not include much of what we consider to be spoilers, such as that Darth Vader is Luke Skywalker's father.) In some cases, the spoilers were given in a brief paragraph prior to the beginning of the story, and in other cases, the spoilers were incorporated into the opening paragraph of the story. There were twelve stories total (four in each genre),[2] and each subject read three stories: one without spoilers, one with the pre-story spoiler paragraph, and one with the opening paragraph spoiler. Finally, subjects were asked to rate how pleasurable they found the stories on a 1–10 scale, with 10 being the greatest amount of pleasure, and 1 being the lowest.

The results were consistent across the board. With respect to all three types of stories, subjects preferred

---

[1] *Psychological Science* 22:9 (September 2011
) <http://journals.sagepub.com/doi/abs/10.1177/0956797611417007>.

[2] The ironic twist stories were: "A Dark Brown Dog," "The Occurrence at Owl Creek Bridge," "The Bet," and "Lamb to the Slaughter." The mystery stories were "Blitzed," "A Chess Problem," "McHenry's Gift," and "Rhyme Never Pays." The literary stories were "The Calm," "Good Dog," "Plumbing," and "Up at a Villa."

the spoiled stories more than the unspoiled stories. Leavitt and Christenfeld speculated that the reason that the subjects preferred the spoiled stories to the unspoiled stories may have to do with the aesthetic pleasure that comes from knowing what is coming in a story and the ease of processing information when one is expecting it.

In an influential article in *Wired*, which reported on Leavitt's and Christenfeld's data, Jonah Lehrer maintains that we actually prefer knowing what will happen in a story, and that we prefer our stories to be predictable (for instance, the bad guy gets caught in the end, the couple in question eventually end up together, the protagonist doesn't die), and that the surprise ending is historically a very recent development.[3] He points out that surprises tend to be more fun for the planner than the one who is surprised, stating

> Our first reaction is almost never "How cool! I never saw that coming!" Instead, we feel embarrassed by our gullibility, the dismay of a prediction error. While authors and screenwriters might enjoy composing those clever twists, they should know that the audience will enjoy it far less.

He goes on to suggest that genres actually constitute a kind of spoiler. People choose to watch a Western, for example, because they want to see John Wayne win the gun fight in the end. Regardless of the reasons, the results of this study are generally seen as shocking to those who hold the view that spoiling is a bad thing, as it is somewhat commonly held that spoiling diminishes pleasure.

---

[3] <https://www.wired.com/2011/08/spoilers-dont-spoil-anything>.

Are the Social Scientists Right?

What should we make of this study? As Dr. Ali Mattu points out on his psychology of fiction blog, *Brain Knows Better*, the methods employed by Leavitt and Christenfeld were generally solid.[4] Still, there are some concerns worth discussing regarding the implications of their research on the question of whether it is bad to spoil.

First, the sample size is sufficiently large for a study of this type, but it is not overwhelmingly large. A considerably larger study might not have produced the same results.

Second, it was limited to short stories. There may be features of short stories that differ significantly from other forms of entertainment, such that it is not clear that a similar study regarding television programs or movies or comic books would yield the result that spoilers don't adversely affect enjoyment.

Third, there may be an issue with the aggregate numbers. While overall the spoiled stories yielded more pleasure than the unspoiled stories, it's not clear that people generally enjoyed the unspoiled stories more. It may be the case, for example, that half the folks strongly disliked having the stories spoiled, while the other half loved the spoiled stories just slightly more than the others hated having the stories spoiled. This would create the illusion that everyone liked all the stories somewhat, but had a slight preference for spoiled stories.

Finally, and most importantly, knowing an ending might not affect enjoyment, in the way that knowing other spoilers might. For example, had I known the ending of the *Harry Potter* series, namely, that *Harry Potter* ultimately defeats Voldemort, it likely would not have

---

[4] <http://brainknowsbetter.com/news/2013/5/11/3-reasons-why-the-psychology-of-spoilers-is-wrong>.

adversely affected my enjoyment of the books at all. Echoing Jonah Lehrers's point above, I certainly could have predicted it. On the other hand, it strikes me that had I been informed that Snape killed Dumbledore in *Harry Potter and the Half-Blood Prince*, my enjoyment of that moment (and the next few weeks where I spent several hours obsessively replaying in my head—I'm still not quite over it) would have been considerably diminished.

This doesn't entail that there is anything wrong with Leavitt's and Christenfeld's conclusions, but, rather, at minimum, further studies are required before we can draw the broader conclusion that spoilers don't actually spoil anything.

So, What if the Social Scientists Are Right?

Putting those concerns aside, let's grant for the sake of argument that knowing spoilers in advance doesn't diminish pleasure, and, in fact, may actually increase it. Even if Leavitt and Christenfeld are correct on this point, it doesn't get us to the conclusion that bears most greatly on our present concern—the question of whether spoiling is bad. There is an important distinction to be made between something coming with less pleasure than one of its alternatives and something being bad in virtue of it. This raises the question can spoiling be bad if the person for whom it is spoiled doesn't have a worse experience because of that thing being spoiled?

---

[5] This example is not as far-fetched as it might seem. There is an Indian restaurant that I sometimes go to, where I place my order, and usually get exactly what I ordered, but about ten percent of the time the chef (who is also the owner) delivers something different. He'll tell me that he thought I would enjoy the special he just made. Most of the time I really like what he has prepared, but my preference is that he never do this.

The answer is that it is not obviously the case that it can't. If spoiling something always (or almost always) resulted in the reader's having a worse experience, then it would be easy to make the case that spoiling is bad. It would be a slam dunk. Leavitt's and Christenfeld's research, however, blocks that move. But there may be other ways in which something can be bad. Consider the following example. Suppose that you have made a nice, but not outstanding, dessert for yourself (perhaps, a bowl of chocolate pudding). Suppose that I come along and take your nice dessert, and replace it with an even nicer dessert (perhaps a chocolate mousse). We can even add to the equation that you much prefer chocolate mousse to chocolate pudding (seriously, no rational person over the age of, say, five, could possibly prefer chocolate pudding to chocolate mousse). Finally, suppose that you eat the chocolate mousse and your pleasure is significantly greater than it would have been had you consumed the pudding. You may well thank me for this. On the other hand, you may be upset that I did it without asking you first. You might not have wanted me to make the decision for you, nor would you want me to take the choice out of your hands.[5] In addition to having positive or pleasurable experiences, we value making our own choices.

Why Spoiling Is Bad

So, one reason for thinking that revealing spoilers might be bad, even in cases in which the revealing of spoilers does not diminish one's pleasure, is that doing so violates the autonomy of the person for whom the work is spoiled. If you know that I'm going to see a good mystery or whodunit, say, for example, *Red Sparrow*, and you reveal the big surprise to me (that the mole is General Vladimir Andreievich Korchnoi), you've deprived me of the choice to see that film spoiler free. Generally, if you tell me in advance that there is a good twist, and ask me if I'd like to know it, and, perhaps, even argue that knowing it will increase my pleasure, but leave the decision up to me, it is likely that I will decline. I would likely choose to experience the movie on my own terms, even if I believe you that I may enjoy it more, if I know the spoiler in advance. So, in cases such as these, there is a demonstrable badness associated with spoiling: it violates autonomy.

A second reason for thinking that spoiling is bad has to do with parties other than the spoiler and the person for whom the work is spoiled. Recall Hitchcock's admonition at the end of *Psycho*, that it not be revealed that Norman Bates is Mother. To the extent that someone spoils the ending for others, Hitchcock's desire goes unsatisfied. While artists don't have a *prima facie* (meaning "at first glance") right to have all their desires satisfied (consider, for example, a filmmaker who desires to have her movie gross $500,000,000, certainly, we don't have an obligation to see that such a desire ever gets fulfilled), if their desires are reasonable and related to how the work of art is experienced, we can see spoilings such as these being bad for the director.

It's not unreasonable for artists to expect their work to be experienced, especially, when the work involves a narrative structure, as they created it. This, requires, among other things, that information be revealed at particular points in time (as the artist intended). Related to this is the idea that a particular consumer of a work of entertainment, may have the desire to experience the entertainment, precisely as the filmmaker intended. Mattu puts this point as follows, "I love walking into a movie without any knowledge of what's going to happen. It's not about the plot—it's about going on the journey the filmmakers intended." Under these circumstances, when a particular work gets spoiled, both the filmmaker and the consumer are harmed, and it's not relevant that the consumer might have enjoyed the work more if they had experienced it differently (for example, with foreknowledge of who committed the crime or whether the guy gets the girl (or *vice versa*)).

A third reason for thinking that spoiling is bad is that it literally spoils one type of experience. The conclusion of the Leavitt-Christenfeld study is that story spoiling doesn't spoil. There are two senses of "spoiling" at play here: "spoiling" as ruining an experience (by depriving the potential experience of that experience) and "spoiling" as ruining the fun associated with the experience. I take it that Leavitt and Christenfeld intend their title to convey both of these senses. The title of their paper could be interpreted as asserting something akin to "ruining someone's experience by revealing a spoiler doesn't ruin someone's fun." This is taken to be correct because their study shows that pleasure actually increases when one is in possession of spoilers in advance. This, I believe rests on a mistake. While having something spoiled might actually lead to an increase in your viewing or reading pleasure, you're not having the same instance of fun. Going back to the pudding metaphor, having a better culinary experience eating mousse doesn't entail that, in doing so, you had the good experience of eating pudding.

Suppose for the sake of argument that I tell you that I'm planning on reading Agatha Christie's *Murder on the Orient Express* and you inform me that it's really great

---

[6] Notice that in this case, the spoiler is something that is revealed in the show very early in the episode. So the benefit that I get from knowing this in advance is negligible, but I have all the negative effects of having it spoiled—I get upset, I don't get to experience as the show's producers and writers intended, I have my autonomy violated, and so on.

because pretty much all the suspects participate in the murder. I can easily imagine that having that knowledge in advance could be a good thing. For example, I might pick up on very subtle details about each character and their motivations as I read, or I might even come to have a greater overall understanding of the work than I would have, had you not spoiled it for me.

Still, the pleasure that I'm having is not the same pleasure I would have had. It's a completely different pleasure, in virtue of being a different experience altogether. Your spoiling the book for me deprived me of that particular pleasure—the pleasure that I would have experienced upon hearing the twist without foreknowledge of it. Moreover, it's a particular pleasure that I can never have, once the work is spoiled. On the other hand, the pleasure that I would get from reading the story with the foreknowledge that each suspect participated in the crime (and all the benefits described above) is still available to me after reading the book unspoiled for the first time. I can always re-read the novel, looking for those subtle clues, and interesting character details. So, having greater amounts of pleasure doesn't entail that there is no loss of pleasure. The pleasure lost is just replaced by a greater pleasure, but a greater pleasure that would have still been available to me, even under circumstances in which I had read the book unspoiled first. Spoiling in these types of cases, does, in fact, come with a badness, and, contrary to the conclusions of Leavitt and Christenfeld, it is a badness that is captured by pleasure lost.

A final reason for thinking that spoilers are bad lies in the fact spoilers upset people—they really upset people! As we've seen when things are spoiled for folks, they exhibit all sorts of behaviors associated with having had a bad experience—they rant, they vent, they lash out, on occasion they stab others in the chest, and so on. This bears on the calculus of the amount of pleasure they experience relevant to viewing a particular show or reading a particular book. It's one thing to ask someone to read or watch something that contains a spoiler and then measure the degree of pleasure that they experience, and subsequently compare that to others watching or reading the same thing who have not had it spoiled. Under controlled circumstances such as these, the spoiler likely won't induce any of the ire that is normally associated with having something spoiled. It's quite another thing, however, when calculating the total pleasure experienced by someone who has had something spoiled outside of controlled experiences. Under these circumstances, the net amount of pleasure that the experience yields relevant to engaging a particular work of entertainment is a function of all the things that go into the experience. These would include both the increase in pleasure from the things detailed in the Leavitt-Christenfeld study (such as paying more attention to the subtleties in plot and character development) that increase the consumer's pleasure, but would also include the anger, frustration, and disappointment that the consumer experiences upon having something spoiled. In a high percentage of cases the net pleasure in cases where things are spoiled is going to be substantially lower than in cases where things are not spoiled. If, for example, I'm waiting to find out whether Chuck dies in the fire that he starts on the Season Three finale of *Better Call Saul* and you tell me that it's revealed in the Season Four premiere, the anger that I experience upon receiving this news is more than sufficient to outweigh any increase in pleasure I receive from knowing this in advance.[6]

So why didn't the Leavitt-Christenfeld experiment track this? In short, it's because they weren't necessarily having people read things that they didn't want spoiled.

In their experiment the subjects were just asked to read things that were almost chosen at random (except for the fact that then needed to be from their three genres). When people get really upset at having something spoiled for them, it is usually an instance of something that they are emotionally invested in: it's a television show that they were looking forward to watching, or possibly a book in a series that they've been reading, or a movie that they've waiting for a long time to see, and so on. People spend a great deal of time anticipating the kinds of experiences that they will have when they see the Season Two finale of *Westworld* or Marvel's follow up to *Avengers: Infinity War*. It's very disappointing to anticipate a certain kind of experience, and to have that experience taken away before you actually get to have it (even under circumstances where the experience is replaced by something that is ultimately good). It seems clear that if Leavitt and Christenfeld had tracked people who were, of their own volition, going to see *Avengers: Infinity War* and had spoiled it for some and not for others, and had asked each to give a pleasure rating of their total experience (enjoyment of the film plus enjoyment of their anticipation of the film), their conclusions would be quite different.

Given that spoiling can be bad for reasons that don't have to do with pleasure (for example, when it deprives individuals of choices that they prefer to make for themselves), that it can be bad for people other than the ones who have things spoiled (for example filmmakers or writers who wish their art to be experienced in certain ways), that it deprives individuals from experiencing works of art in the ways in which they are intended, that it permanently deprives people of particular pleasures, and, most importantly, that it can cause great anger, frustration, and consternation, we cannot help but conclude that many (perhaps even most) instances of spoiling are bad. This is not to say that the results of the Leavitt-Christenfeld study aren't interesting or accurate, they just fail to capture features of spoiling that are ubiquitous outside of their controlled setting.

7
The Badness of Spoiling

In the previous chapter we established that, despite what the social scientists tell us, spoiling can be bad. A logical next step is to attempt to locate that badness. To some extent we've already done this. We've seen that spoiling can deprive one of pleasure or violate someone's autonomy. But there are many other ways in which spoiling can be bad. So, what are the ways in which spoiling can be bad? Or to be more precise, what are the sources of the badness of spoiling?

Do the Great Moral Philosophers Have Anything Useful to Say about Spoilers?

A natural place to begin, if we're attempting to give an account of why something might be thought to be unethical, is to see what the great moral philosophers have to say about it. In particular, we might want to examine the classic theories of normative ethics and apply the conclusions of those theories to some particular issue, such as whether spoiling is bad, and if so, determine precisely why it's bad. Let's call this the "Ethical Theory Approach."

For example, we might take a look at Utilitarianism as presented by either Jeremy Bentham or John Stuart Mill, which holds that we should always do what we can to maximize happiness for the greatest number of people, and see what it has to say about the revealing of spoilers. Similarly, we could look at the various formulations of Kant's Categorical Imperative, which maintains that people should only act on maxims that they could unproblematically will to be a universal law (according to one formulation), or that people should not use others as mere means to an end, as opposed to treating others as ends in themselves (according to a different formulation), and then see what particular verdicts are issued with respect to spoilers.

The same could be done with Aristotle's Virtue Theory, W. D. Ross's Intuitionism, and Nel Noddings's Care Ethics, and so forth. A virtue of this approach is that, if successful, it not only identifies the locus of the badness of spoiling (for instance, spoiling is bad because it is not what the perfectly virtuous agent would do), it directly ties the fact of the badness to the ethics of spoiling. That is, because of its running afoul of the ethical theory, the act of spoiling must be bad.

While the Ethical Theory Approach is both natural and commonplace when philosophers engage in applied ethical analysis, I think it is best to resist this strategy for a number of reasons. First, while these theories are very good at capturing aspects of morally correct and morally bad behavior, each tends to be somewhat wrong. That is, each of these theories admits of numerous counterexamples—cases in which each renders the wrong, and occasionally horrific, verdict. Kant's moral theory at times justifies killing (if the situation is described just right), Mill's theory justifies (under certain circumstances) slavery, and so forth. Second, these theories are laid out in such a way as to be mutually exclusive, so at most only one of them is correct. Third, it's not clear that they will be applicable to spoilers in an interesting and nuanced way. For example, Utilitarianism, in its simplicity, will simply hold that spoiling is impermissible only if doing so fails to maximize happiness. Care Ethics and Virtue Theory, are even more difficult to apply to the topic of spoilers. Virtue Theory, for example, would hold that revealing spoilers is okay if it is done by someone virtuous, and not okay if it is done by someone who is not virtuous, even if all other details in a particular situation are held constant. Fourth, there is nothing in these theories that suggests that we will end up with our desired equilibrium between what our account of spoilers says and what ordinary non-philosophers are inclined to say about the badness of spoiling (again, failure to do this should constitute a huge red flag).

Finally, and perhaps most importantly, while these accounts link the badness of spoiling to the ethics of spoiling, they do so in the wrong way. What they render is an account of the badness of spoiling that derives from what their theory says about the impermissibility of spoiling. This results in a pretty trivial, and, ultimately, not particularly elucidating, relationship between the ethics of spoiling and the badness of spoiling. It's as if they are saying something runs afoul of their theory so *ipso facto* it must be bad. This is getting things exactly backwards. Ideally, we want to derive the impermissibility of spoiling from the badness of it, and not the other way around. Related to this is the fact that any theory that attempts to boil morality down to a single principle (such as that morality is just a matter of maximizing happiness) will likely not be able to account for the manifold ways in which spoiling can be bad.[1] That spoiling (on one account) leads to diminished pleasure, or that it (on another account) violates autonomy, is worth noting, and is certainly part of a complete account of the badness of spoiling, but neither of these things, nor any other single source of badness, will by themselves tell the entire story. For these reasons, it's best to focus on the ways in which spoiling can be bad, and then 1. give an account of the badness of spoiling, and 2. check to see whether the account of the badness that we give jibes with our common-sense intuitions about what constitutes a spoiler. Once we've done that we can attempt to link the badness of spoiling with the ethics of spoiling.

Perhaps a Little Death Might Prove Useful

While we will not be relying directly on the wisdom of the great moral philosophers to locate the badness of spoiling, we can still draw on some well thought out philosophy (some of which is clearly informed and inspired by the greats!). Those philosophers who work on the metaphysics of death, for example, have much to offer that is useful for our purposes regarding the nature of badness.

One reason that the literature on the badness of death is relevant to the ethics of spoilers is that death is not something that is experienced by the person who dies, and some of the badness of spoiling has to do with experiences not had.[2] There is an age-old philosophical puzzle regarding the

---

[1] W.D. Ross's Intuitionism fares a little better in this respect, as it identifies seven *prima facie* moral duties (reparation, fidelity, gratitude, justice, beneficence, non-maleficence, and self-improvement), which correspond to seven ways in which badness can result (he does allow, however, that there may be others), but, as we'll see, even those will not be able to account for all the ways in which spoiling can be bad.

[2] In the literature on the metaphysics of death it is taken as a given that there is not an afterlife. Death, rather, is a state of non-existence—an

badness of death, which stems from the idea that when you are dead, you no longer exist, so it is never the case that your death can be bad for you.[3] If death is simply the cessation of life and nothing more, then it is not clear why death is thought to be a bad thing. Epicurus puts it like this: "Death is nothing to us, since when we are, death has not come, and when death has come, we are not."[4] If death is considered to be an experiential blank, then the badness of death cannot be accounted for in terms of some sort of unpleasant experience; the badness of death must lie elsewhere. This requires that theorists who maintain that death is bad for the person who dies elucidate the ways in which something can be bad for someone, even if the dead person does not experience that badness themselves.

A number of accounts of the badness of death have been offered over the years, but two seem particularly relevant to our discussion: Thomas Nagel's Deprivation account and Bernard Williams's Desire Frustration account.[5] The Deprivation view maintains that the badness of death lies in its depriving persons of the good things that life has to offer (Nagel calls these good things

---

experiential blank. Of course, not everyone holds this view. This doesn't, however, bear on the legitimacy of the claims being made. Think of these arguments as asking "If death were an experiential blank, what would be bad about death?"

[3] There is a second argument for the view that death is not bad for the person who dies, which goes as follows: since we don't consider the time before we exist to be bad, and that time is metaphysically identical to the time after we die (each involves non-existence), then the time after we die (that is, death) should not be considered a bad thing either.

[4] Epicurus, "Letter to Menoeceus," 124b–127a, in *Epicurus: Letters Principal Doctrines, and Vatican Sayings*, edited by Russel M. Greer (Upper Saddle River: Prentice Hall, 1997).

[5] See Thomas Nagel, "Death," in his *Mortal Questions* (Cambridge: Cambridge University Press, 1979), and Bernard Williams, "The Makropulos Case: Reflections on the Tedium of Immortality," in his *Problems of the Self* (Cambridge: Cambridge University Press, 1973).

"the *praemia vitae*"). Obviously, if you're dead you don't get the good things that you would have had, had you not died. The Desire Frustration view is the position that death is bad insofar as it frustrates certain of our important desires. Similarly, if you're dead, at least some of your desires—those that are contingent on one still being alive at some future time—are never satisfied.[6]

Let's apply salient aspects of each of these views to spoilers. A Deprivation view of the badness of revealing spoilers would hold that at least part of the badness of having something spoiled lies in the fact that the person for whom the work was spoiled was deprived of some good thing. Generally, that good thing would be something like the experience of encountering a particular work of art unspoiled. In particular instances this can be cashed out in a number of different ways. One could, for instance, be denied an "Oh my gosh, I didn't see that coming" moment, such as the ending of *The Usual Suspects*, where Kevin Spacey's character (Verbal Kint) had been Keyser Söze the whole time. Or one could miss the pleasure that comes with engaging an unspoiled story where the viewer spends much time wondering things such as "How are they going to get out of this?" and then learns how it resolves itself. The much loved "Battle of the Bastards" episode of *Game of Thrones* is a good example of this phenomenon. If one had been told in advance that just as things appeared beyond hope for Jon Snow's army, The Vale Army would arrive to help bring about Snow's victory (and Ramsay's defeat!), one would not have experienced all the tension and drama that made the episode so fun

---

[6] Of course, not all desires are of this kind. Satisfaction of my desire for my son to be successful after graduating from college is not contingent on my being alive at that time, whereas, satisfaction of my desire to celebrate my next birthday is contingent on my being alive on my next birthday.

to watch. These are just a couple of examples. No doubt there are countless more things one could be deprived of by knowing significant plot details in advance.

The Desire Frustration view of the badness of revealing spoilers, as the name suggests, would hold that at least part of the badness of having spoilers revealed lies in having certain desires frustrated. In the most straightforward of cases, one might simply have a desire to not have something spoiled for them. Certainly, much evidence for this lies in the fact that people will go to great lengths to avoid spoilers, or they will admonish people not to spoil particular things for them, or they will lash out (or worse!) at people who have spoiled something for them. But there are other desires more specific to the plot that may get frustrated when something is spoiled, as well. For example, someone might sit down to a good tear jerker (I'm thinking *Old Yeller* here, but that's probably because I haven't intentionally watched a tear jerker since I was seven or eight years old) for the express purpose of having a certain sort of emotional experience. For a lot of people, knowing certain of the particulars is sufficient to adversely affect that experience. I might have heard that something really sad happens in a particular episode of *Buffy the Vampire Slayer*[7] and knowing this may have piqued my interest. I may have even formed a desire to watch the episode for just this event, and in some sense, looked forward to experiencing the sadness. On the other hand, had the person gone on to tell me that at the end of the episode Warren kills Tara,[8] my enjoyment would have been somewhat diminished, and my desire to fully enjoy that development would have been nearly completely

---

[7] Apropos of our earlier discussion on vagueness, this might rise to the level of a spoiler, but for convenience sake I'll ignore this for the moment.

[8] I gotta admit, I'm still kind of sad about this one.

frustrated. There are no doubt countless other desires each of which involve experiencing a work or art unspoiled that could be frustrated. For example, part of the joy of watching slasher films is predicting at the beginning, which characters will survive and in which order they die, etc. Something similar can be said about whodunnits and crime thrillers, where the fun lies in trying to crack the case before it's revealed who committed the crime. One might read a good book or watch a film or program in order to get "lost in the experience." It's not difficult to see how spending reading or viewing time wondering when a spoiler that has been revealed to them is going to occur could distract from their doing so, and in turn frustrate their desire. In short, people have lots of desires related to their engaging works of entertainment, which could easily be thwarted having those works spoiled.

As was mentioned in the previous chapter, it's not just the person who experiences a work of art who has desires about whether that work gets spoiled. People involved with the production of a movie, book, or television program will frequently have strong desires that works not be spoiled (recall the admonitions at the end of *The Mousetrap*, *Psycho*, and *Les Diaboliques*). Certainly writers, directors, and actors have a vested interested in how their art is received. Such desires may stem from concerns related to artistic vision, but they need not. If enough people spoil a whodunit, for example, it could affect ratings or box office revenues, which, in turn, could affect their ability to have future projects funded or future books published, and so forth. So, in some cases, revealing spoilers can have pretty significant consequences.

Bad Experiences

It seems right to say that deprivation and desire frustration account for the lion's share of the badness that occurs when something is spoiled. This makes sense. When someone spoils a work for someone the thing that seems most salient is that something has been taken from that person, or they ultimately have a desire that goes unfulfilled. In many cases it is both at once (deprivation and desire frustration are often two sides of the same coin—we might have a desire not to be deprived of some particular thing). That said, not far behind deprivation and desire frustration lies the bad experience that goes along with having something spoiled. As has been pointed out several times already, people can have pretty strong reactions to spoilers. A reaction to having something spoiled might range from being a little pissed off or mildly perturbed at one end of the spectrum to being downright furious or having feelings of hostility at the other end (one might even become so enraged that they stab someone in the chest). It feels bad to have something spoiled.[9] We might experience great frustration upon encountering a spoiler.[10]

While a complete taxonomy of the sorts of bad experiences that we may have in virtue of having something spoiled is beyond the scope of this book, we can identify enough of the ways in which spoiling can be experientially bad to provide a general sense of the extent to which the badness occurs. We've already mentioned that varying degrees of anger might result from a spoiling, and have also mentioned feelings of frustration. Additionally, we might feel that we had wasted the time we had already invested in the show, book, or film series. We may feel that we had

---

[9] See Appendix 2 for several real-life examples of how people felt upon having something spoiled.

[10] Note that this is a different sense of the word "frustration" than is employed in the expression "desire frustration." In the current sense "frustration" refers to a psychological state—a particular unpleasant way that we might feel. Conversely, when we're discussing desire frustration, "frustration" means something like "thwarted" or "unrealized."

wasted money (given that we're not going to get the complete experience). We may feel sad that we missed out on a particular experience (we can think of this as the badness, or the set of bad feelings, that goes along with recognizing that we've been deprived of something or that we have a desire that will certainly go unfulfilled). We might just experience a general feeling of remorse. Perhaps we experience remorse for having something spoiled, or remorse for investing much time and energy into something that gets spoiled, or remorse for not having avoided spoilers, etc.[11] The list goes on and on. Having something spoiled can lead to our having a very bad experience.

Related to the idea of something being bad in virtue of the experience we have is the idea that something can be bad in virtue of its comparison to alternative experiences we might have had. For example, something can be thought of as having a kind of badness associated with it if the experience that we have is worse than the experience we would have had under different circumstances. We can call this sort of badness "comparative badness."

Comparative badness need not involve comparison of experiences. For instance, Policy A might be worse than Policy B, if Policy A deprives a group of people of more of some social good (such as opportunities or dignity) than

---

[11] I've experienced remorse for not having avoided spoilers on a number of occasions. Typically, it happens with shows that I've recorded to watch later. There are a handful of shows, in particular, that people on social media are liable to discuss: *The Walking Dead*, *Game of Thrones*, and *Westworld*. *Breaking Bad*, when it was still airing, was one of these shows. One of these shows will air. I will be planning on watching it in an hour or two. Without thinking I'll pop on Facebook, and there it will be: The death list from the Red Wedding or Dolores killed Arnold or Jon Snow is not still dead. When this happens, I'm usually pretty mad at whichever of my friends posted the spoiler, but I'm really upset with myself for not avoiding social media. I know better (or at least I think I know better, though my behavior might tend to suggest otherwise).

Policy B deprives them of. But for our purposes comparisons of experiences will render another type of badness of spoilers.

Here's the idea. If spoiling something leads to a worse experience for a particular person, than some other experience they would have had if that work had not been spoiled for them, then we can say that spoiling the work is bad in the sense of being comparatively bad.[12] Note that for something to be comparatively worse than something else, it does not have to be bad; it just hast to be worse than the state of affairs it is being compared to. Suppose for example that you tell me that in *Twin Peaks*, Laura Palmer's killer is some guy named Bob, and that Bob was inhabiting Leland Palmer's body at the time of the killing. Also suppose that I watch *Twin Peaks* with this knowledge and still have a great viewing experience. That doesn't entail that your revealing the spoilers to me wasn't comparatively bad. As long as I would have had an even better experience had you not spoiled it, it still can be seen as bad.

The Leavitt-Christenfeld study discussed in Chapter 6 was tacitly employing a notion of comparative badness. Their argument seemed to boil down to: 1. everyone thinks that spoilers are bad, but 2. the research seems to show that on average people report having better experiences when

---

[12] Allow me to illustrate what I'm talking about with a real life example that is actually about the very point I'm making. If I had written the sentence in which this footnote appears when I was just out of graduate school, it undoubtedly would have involved several pages about the nature of counterfactual propositions, what constitutes a close possible world, a discussion of how to conceive of possible worlds (Lewis/Stalnaker vs. Kripke) and whatever else I was thinking about modal metaphysics at the time. Regarding the experience of the reader, comparatively this would have been much worse than the experience you had reading the short sentence I went with here. You're welcome!

things are spoiled, so 3. in virtue of how the comparisons come out, spoiling is not bad. Since we've already evaluated their claims, we won't rehash the discussion here, except to say that if it turns out that on average spoiling is worse, comparatively, than non-spoiling, then spoiling is bad. The same considerations might also apply to personal spoilers, but there one wouldn't need to look at averages.

Other Ways in which Spoilers May Be Bad

Taking stock, we see that up to this point we've seen that spoiling can be bad in virtue of both things experienced by the person for whom the work is spoiled, such as the way that person might feel upon having something spoiled, and things not experienced, such as the person being deprived of something good. We've also seen that the badness of spoiling is not restricted to the person who encounters the spoiler. The badness of spoiling might also fall on the creator of a work, even if that person is not aware that a spoiler was revealed. Let's now consider some of the other ways in which spoiling can be bad.

In the previous chapter we discussed violations of autonomy. Recall that something can be bad for someone if it restricts their autonomy. Here things can get a bit tricky. One common defense that persons who spoil provide is also based on autonomy. Take my aforementioned friend Cassandra. Recall that she frequently reveals spoilers on social media whenever a character that she likes from *The Walking Dead* dies or becomes undead.[13] Some percentage of the time, when admonished for spoiling, she responds that she is exercising her right to free speech, and consequently she has a right to do so.

---

[13] Or both. You pretty much have to die first in order to become undead, at least as far as zombies are concerned. Vampire metaphysics are more complicated.

One response to this defense is to point out that her right to free speech is a legal right, but, of course, all things legal are not moral.[14] This response, however, does not get at the heart of the issue. If our concern is that revealing spoilers violates autonomy, then it is incumbent upon us to provide a rationale as to why the autonomy of spoiler revealers, such as Cassandra, should be violated instead. As much as people don't enjoy having things spoiled, some who routinely spoil things for others really enjoy revealing spoilers, and choose to exercise their autonomy doing just that.

Note that autonomy is a form of liberty—it is the right to choose for yourself what you will do. Generally speaking, moral and political philosophers who write about liberty (such as Locke, Marx, or Rawls) hold that the right to exercise liberty only extends as far as others having compatible rights. This means that I have liberty (and by extension legitimate governments will recognize that liberty) only to the extent that my exercising of my liberty does not infringe on the liberty of others. So when Cassandra posted a picture of Shane from *The Walking Dead* on Facebook the night that he was killed by Rick (along with "OMG!!!" and a dozen or so emojis meant to express both shock and utter despair), her acting autonomously (and exercising her liberty) violated my autonomy (and thus restricted my liberty).[15] So in situations such as these, where the autonomy of two persons comes into

---

[14] Legally speaking, people have the right to call others names, to body shame, to express racist or sexist or homophobic or transphobic viewpoints, etc. That doesn't diminish moral wrongness of doing so.

[15] The fact that this happened on social media may be relevant in ways not brought up in this chapter. We will revisit the Cassandra case again in Chapter 10. Spoiler Alert! Because her transgressions occurred on regular Facebook, as opposed to a Comic-Con Facebook page, the verdict on her actions will not change.

conflict, if it turns out that one person exercising their autonomy will restrict the autonomy of the other, but not *vice versa,* then the person restricting the autonomy of the other is not exercising a moral right that they actually have—their behavior exceeds what the right to autonomy grants them.

Related to this is the fact that in many cases revealing spoilers violates the Golden Rule, which states "Do unto others as you would have them do unto you." The Golden Rule serves to identify an important constraint on a person's liberty. Since most folks would not want to have things spoiled for them, they are obligated to not spoil things for others. Of course, famously, the Golden Rule fails (at least on the face of things) for those who don't mind having certain things done to them, even if most folks would consider those things bad. A slight modification involving our typical viewer standard will yield the right result. Regarding spoilers, we should do unto others as a typical viewer would want us to do unto them.

Finally, in addition to the badness that spoiling has for the person on the receiving end of the spoiler and the badness that it has for the creators of works of art or entertainment, it is also the case that spoiling can be bad for the person who does the spoiling. One of the things that the Virtue Theorists, such as Aristotle, get right is that it is important that we develop good characters if we are going to flourish as individuals. Occasionally inadvertently revealing spoilers, or even occasionally doing so on purpose, will likely not bear much on character development. On the other hand, being a more than occasional or even a frequent spoiler revealer, whether doing so stems from a desire to spoil other people's fun or stems from a blatant disregard for the wishes of others, is precisely the sort of thing that can inhibit character growth. Not caring about the wishes and well-being of others (again, either out of malice or a general disregard for the concerns and wishes of others) is the sort of thing that perpetuates itself. It becomes easier and easier the more you do it. The way people currently act toward one another on social media is good evidence for this. The type of disrespect for fellow human beings that most of us witness on a daily basis used to be behavior that people found appalling. Now it seems commonplace.[16] To be clear I'm not suggesting that being a spoiler revealer will make you a horrible person, but, at minimum, it certainly isn't doing anything to better yourself, and it may be part of a pattern of behavior that serves to worsen your character. A second reason for thinking that being a spoiler revealer might be bad for the revealer lies in the fact that you just might get punched in the nose (or stabbed in the chest!). As has been pointed out, people really hate having things spoiled.

Linking the Badness of Spoiling to Ethics

So, we've now seen several ways in which spoiling leads to badness. Some ways involve things experienced, and others do not. Furthermore, in some cases spoiling is bad for the person doing the spoiling. In some cases, it's bad for the person who had something spoiled. In some cases, it's bad for someone else altogether. Our final task in this chapter is to link the badness of spoiling to the ethics of spoiling.

We've already discussed one way of doing this, namely, to latch on to a moral theory and see which actions turn out to be permissible and which actions turn out to be impermissible, according to that theory. We called this the

---

[16] I'm concerned that I'm beginning to sound like one of those people who say stuff, such as "Back in my day . . ." I don't think that's what going on here. If you disagree I'll just kindly ask you to get off my lawn.

Ethical Theory Approach. We had a number of reasons for rejecting this approach, but most important among them was the fact that these theories link badness and ethics in the wrong way. Our plan was to identify the sources of badness associated with spoiling, and derive our ethical obligations from those sources. This will happen with greater specificity over the next two chapters, but we can draw a preliminary general conclusion about the relationship between spoiling and ethics here. To the extent that something yields badness, it is *prima facie* unethical. I say *prima facie* here because there might be all sorts of circumstances that arise that would render this false in those circumstances. For example, if I were to find myself in a situation in which all my options for acting would result in badness, but there were one action that would clearly lead to the least amount of badness, then it would not (in most such cases) be unethical for me to choose that action.[17] Similarly if I were to find myself in a situation where violating someone's autonomy might prevent greater harms or rights violations from occurring, then my action would not be unethical.[18] As we will see, there are countless other cases in which exceptions arise. Yet, *prima facie*, spoiling, in virtue of the many ways in which it leads to badness, is unethical.

---

[17] The philosophical literature on applied ethics is chockfull of examples of this phenomenon. Consider the famous trolley problem or any number of rescue cases in which to save a greater number of people you have to let someone die, where letting someone die is viewed as a bad thing.

[18] Here I have in mind the sort of case where someone is about to suffer some great injury, so someone else acts on their behalf. For example, Person A states that he wants to stand in a particular spot on the sidewalk, and Person B upon seeing that a piano is falling from above, pushes Person A against their will to safety out of their desired spot.

8
When Is It Wrong to Spoil?

W e've now established that revealing spoilers can lead
to badness for a variety of reasons. In some instances,
spoiling leads to someone being deprived of certain goods,
such as the experience of viewing or reading something
unspoiled. In other instances, it leads to desires being
frustrated, such as the desire to not have your artistic
work spoiled for those who have yet to encounter it or the
desire to see something unspoiled, yourself.

Spoiling can also lead to varieties of phenomenological
or experiential badness, such as feelings of remorse or
anger or frustration, and so forth. It can be bad in virtue
of a sort of comparative badness obtaining, in which the
particular experience that one has upon viewing or reading something is not as good (even if it is still a positive
experience) as the experience one would have had, had
they encountered the work unspoiled. Finally, in some
cases it can lead to rights violations, such as the right to
autonomy or liberty (and violations of the Golden Rule).
Furthermore, the badness of spoiling can fall on the person for whom the work is spoiled, the person who did the
spoiling, or the creators of the work of art (and likely

many others!).[1] We might be tempted to conclude on the basis of all this that you should *never* reveal spoilers. As a guiding principle, that is not the worst way to go, and it is generally good to err on the side of caution.[2] Still to conclude that you should never spoil would be too hasty, and while erring on the side of caution works nicely as a guiding principle, it won't provide an accurate account of just when it is wrong to spoil, nor will it allow us to account for the more interesting nuanced cases that we will consider in Chapters 8 and 9. What is called for, then, is something more precise.

When Is It Clearly Okay to Spoil?

We've already discussed one reason for thinking that a universal prohibition on revealing spoilers does not exist, namely, that it is okay for trailers to reveal spoilers.[3] Recall that we held that the fact that people expected to have significant information revealed in trailers was considered to be morally relevant. It was also considered to be morally relevant that people could, without much effort, avoid seeing them. Finally, we argued that having trailers that revealed significant information was a cost of having a great many high-budget movies released each year. Similarly, having trailers that reveal spoilers for television programs is a cost of having high-quality television programs.[4] So even though watching a trailer might result in

---

[1] Consider the case of the man who is so upset by a spoiling, that he kicks the family dog out of anger. While the dog kicker is morally responsible for his actions, it is nevertheless plausible to assert that some of the badness of spoiling fell on the dog.

[2] If everyone adopted the principle that we should never spoil, I'm convinced that the world would be a much better place.

[3] Of course, there were limits on this. Frequently a trailer will reveal more than is appropriate or warranted.

[4] The fear is that if the high-quality television programs aren't adver-

any of the aforementioned kinds of badness, on balance it's okay for trailers to reveal spoilers.

A second reason for thinking that a universal prohibition on revealing spoilers doesn't exist lies in the fact that in most cases spoilers have a pretty short shelf-life. Recall that in Chapter 3 we saw that once the shelf-life on some bit of information expires, it can no longer be thought of as a spoiler, or at least not thought of as a thing that could be legitimately spoiled. This corresponded with our ordinary usage of the term "spoiler." For example, revealing that in *Sharp Objects* there were two killers, Adora and Amma, is a legitimate spoiler, as it aired very recently (at the time this book was being written), but revealing that in *The Man with Two Brains* the Elevator Killer turned out to be Merv Griffin is not a legitimate spoiler, as it was released about twenty-five years earlier. The upshot of this is that once a bit of information is sufficiently old (provided that it does not pertain to one of the things that can never be spoiled), then it cannot possibly be a spoiler—it is metaphysically precluded by its status from any longer being a spoiler. So why is this being proffered as a counterexample to a universal prohibition on spoilers? If these things are no longer spoilers, it appears that they simply aren't applicable to a discussion of when things can be spoilers.

This "seems" correct, but it raises an interesting question: does a particular bit of information lose its status *as a spoiler* once its shelf-life as a spoiler has expired or is it still a spoiler, just one that it is now okay to reveal? On the one hand, the definition of a spoiler that we finally settled on (SP5) holds that in order to be a spoiler, a work

---

tised extensively we will go back to the days of *Mannix, Holmes and Yo-Yo, The Misadventures of Sheriff Lobo, Cop Rock,* and *The New Leave It to Beaver.*

must not be too old. Thus, by those lights, a particular bit of information loses its spoiler status over time (again, provided that it is not one of those things that can never be spoiled). On the other hand, our ordinary usage of the term "spoiler" is still used to discuss spoilers that have passed their expiration date. Specifically, folks are inclined to refer to "spoilers that it is okay to reveal" or "expired spoilers." So, we have good reason for considering expired spoilers *to be spoilers* in some sense, and we also have good reason for thinking that they are not spoilers.

Perhaps there is a way to thread the needle. If we further revise our notion of a legitimate spoiler[5] in such a way as to restrict it to just those spoilers that it is *prima facie* wrong to spoil, then we can maintain that expired spoilers are still spoilers—they are just not legitimate spoilers—and that it is not wrong to spoil them. This solution has the virtue of both jibing with our ordinary usage of the term "spoiler," and keeping our theoretical account of spoilers intact.

A third reason for rejecting the idea that a universal prohibition on revealing spoilers exists can be found in our practices (when we are being good citizens) of issuing spoiler alerts. Prefacing one's remarks with a spoiler alert creates a context (in most circumstances) in which the revealing of a spoiler is morally permissible. Of course, it is not quite as simple as that, and we'll discuss the details of spoiler alerts in Chapter 11, but for now we can conclude that in at least some cases, it is okay to reveal legitimate spoilers once a spoiler alert has been issued.

---

[5] Examples of non-legitimate spoilers would include expired spoilers, personal spoilers, and anything that turns out to be generally okay to reveal, but is not okay in certain contexts.

Now that we've established that there does not exist a universal prohibition on revealing spoilers, we can turn our attention to cases in which it is clearly wrong to reveal spoilers.

When Spoiling Is Obviously Wrong

Let's begin with the easy cases. First of all, since there are certain things that we've concluded should never be spoiled, then *prima facie* it would be wrong to reveal any of these things. Recall that this includes both entire works (such as the entire *Harry Potter* book series) as well as particular parts of certain other works (such as the ending of *Planet of the Apes*). The relevant factor here is greatness. We need the qualifier *"prima facie"* because we can easily imagine a circumstance in which some other more important consideration arises that pulls us in the opposite direction. So, we may have an obligation *not to spoil* the ending of *Planet of the Apes*, but at the same time have an even greater obligation *to spoil* it. Under such circumstances it would not be wrong to reveal that the planet of the apes is Earth.[6]

A second class of cases in which it is clearly wrong to reveal spoilers are those that involve the various ways in which spoilers can be bad discussed above (such as desire frustration or deprivation). We've established that when spoilers are revealed, badness can occur in a number of ways for a number of different individuals. Whenever such badness does occur, then it is *prima facie* wrong to reveal spoilers.

A third class of cases in which it is clearly wrong to reveal spoilers are those that involve personal spoilers.

---

[6] I could provide an example here, but since we are going to be discussing these sorts of circumstances in Chapter 9, and Chapter 9 is pretty great—it would be wrong to spoil it for you.

Recall that personal spoilers are spoilers that are not legitimate spoilers, but would still have the effect spoiling something for some particular person. Again, if you know that someone is about watch or read something for the first time and that thing's spoiler shelf life has expired, it would still be *prima facie* wrong to reveal any spoilers pertaining to it to that person.

Some Not So Obvious Cases in which Spoiling May Be Wrong

So much for the easy cases. Now let's consider some trickier situations.

To begin with, we will consider cases in which permission to spoil is granted. We might be inclined to think that it's always okay to reveal a spoiler under such circumstances. Suppose, for example, that someone wants to discuss the ending of *The Happytime Murders* with a friend who hasn't seen it yet, but suggests not discussing it, out of fear of revealing that Sandra is the murderer and that Jenny did not die in the car bombing.[7] We can easily imagine the friend saying "It's okay, I'm not going to see it, you can tell me what happens." In this case, it seems that little or no badness will ensue if the spoiler is revealed. Consequently, it would not be wrong to do so.

Contrast this with the following case. Suppose that someone is binge watching *Breaking Bad*, which they have seen previously, with a friend who is watching it for the first time.[8] Further, suppose that after watching Sea-

---

[7] Usually I go through a fairly lengthy deliberative process when deciding which works to use as examples, but I'm going to level with you here. I watched *The Happytime Murders* last night and it was so horrible that I actually feel traumatized by its awfulness. I'm hoping (but not optimistic) that writing about it will make the pain go away.

[8] You might be thinking that the shelf life for spoilers for *Breaking Bad* must have surely expired by now, and that undermines the example. You

son Three, and seeing that Jesse murders Gale, the friend asks whether Gus retaliates against Walt and Jesse, and makes it clear that he *really* wants to know this, and "just can't wait" until they have a chance to watch the first episode of Season Four. The person who has seen it before has now been given permission to spoil the Season Four opener, but it is not obvious that it's morally okay to do so. On the one hand revealing that Gus does not retaliate is consistent with respecting the autonomy of the friend who wants to have the spoiler revealed. But not telling him is also consistent with respecting his autonomy.

Respecting the autonomy of another doesn't require that we do whatever they desire we do; rather, it requires that we don't prevent them from doing what they desire (with all the caveats about the liberty and autonomy of others discussed above). Moreover, if the friend really wants the information, they can easily look it up on Google or on a fan page or on a wiki. So, at best, not telling them would not be an instance of violating their autonomy. Furthermore, if it's the case that badness would result from their friend telling them, then the friend's obligation to not tell has not been waived.

Clearly, some of the types of badness discussed previously, would not obtain if the spoiler were revealed. For example, there is no reason to suppose that the friend who asked to be told the spoiler would feel anger or frustration upon hearing it. Nor would they have a desire frustrated—their desire to see it unspoiled has been replaced by a desire to know the spoiler in advance of seeing the episode. Still, there would quite likely be badness. Their experience upon watching the Season Four premiere would be diminished, so there is both comparative bad-

---

would be wrong, however, as *Breaking Bad* sits very near the top of those television shows that are so great that they can never be spoiled.

ness and they would be deprived of a positive experience, just to give a couple of examples. The particulars of the circumstances are relevant. In *The Happytime Murders* example, the person who granted permission to hear a spoiler had no emotional investment in the movie, and likely was not on the receiving end of any badness in virtue of hearing the spoiler. Conversely, in the *Breaking Bad* case, the person who wanted to hear the spoiler had a strong emotional investment in the show (their strong desire to have the spoiler revealed is a function of that strong emotional investment), and as a result would have incurred a great deal of badness (relatively speaking) had their request been granted. In cases such as the *Breaking Bad* case, we're justified in taking a paternalistic stance toward the person granting permission to receive a spoiler. If badness is going to be the result of a spoiling, we ought to deny the request for a spoiler, and it should be done for the person's own good.

As stated previously, if they really want the information, they can certainly obtain it, but in a good number of cases, they won't seek it out. This is because the desire to know a spoiler when you "just can't wait" is often a fleeting desire. Typically, in such cases, eventually your more rational and controlled "self" will take over. It's almost as if we're respecting the autonomy of the person by respecting their true wishes when we deny requests that are 1. impulsive, and 2. not in their best interests. An apt analogy is someone who in a moment of weakness asks to be told what they will be receiving for Christmas a day or two in advance of the holiday. Even if they grant permission, we would be doing them a disservice by revealing the information, as their gift opening experience will be diminished.[9]

---

[9] It's worth noting that it is not just children who make such requests.

Another tricky set of cases involves works of entertainment spoiling other works of entertainment. This happens with great frequency. Suppose that you're interested in watching two sporting events that are airing simultaneously. You record one on the DVR and watch the other one live. During the live broadcast they frequently show highlights from the other games, and usually without warning. So, it might be the case that one event is spoiled by the other one. This case is pretty easily resolved. Since it is to be expected (highlights are actually part of the show), it doesn't count as a legitimate spoiler.[10] Almost no one is bothered by this phenomenon, and most fans of sports appreciate seeing what is going on in the other games or matches.

One work of entertainment spoiling another also happens when later episodes of a television program or subsequent movies refer back to the events of previous episodes or earlier films. For example, the events of nearly every episode of Season Eight of *Shameless* refer back to the events of Season Seven episodes (for example, Lip's expulsion from college and ongoing struggles with alcoholism), and many of the events of *The Godfather: Part II* refer back to the events of *The Godfather* (such as Fredo's various betrayals of Michael and the murder of Moe Greene). Again, since this is to be expected, the pieces of information revealed do not count as legitimate spoilers, and no one is bothered by this.[11]

---

[10] The "because it's expected, it's not a legitimate spoiler" criteria works in these types of cases, but I'm not intending this to apply universally. Suppose, for example, that one particular announcer of football games began telling movie spoilers on a weekly basis during *Monday Night Football*. Just because it happened with regularity and people came to expect it, would not make it unobjectionable. The difference between this example, and the ones involving highlights from other games, is that the highlights are welcomed by the viewers.

[11] The closest we get to something of this nature being objectionable is when a film company chooses to make a stand-alone movie from the middle

While these examples are neither objectionable, nor difficult to reconcile with our account of the badness of spoilers, there is a more recent phenomenon, that is a bit troubling. At the end of *Ant-Man and the Wasp* there are two additional scenes—a mid-credits scene, and an end-credits scene. Both reveal spoilers (albeit somewhat vaguely) about *Avengers: Infinity War*. The mid-credits scene shows Hank Pym, Janet Van Dyne, and Hope Van Dyne reduced to ashes in the same fashion that so many characters were at the end of *Infinity War*. The end credits scene showed that subsequent to Thanos snapping his fingers and ridding the universe of half of its population, things were in great disarray on Earth, as is evidenced by the fact that the television networks were no longer airing programming (only a test pattern was being broadcast). Both of these spoilers about the *Avengers* series were revealed while *Avengers: Infinity War* was still in the theaters! People in the audience who had not already seen *Infinity War* had just had the ending spoiled for them.[12]

This raises the question: was it wrong for the Marvel Cinematic Universe folks to have one film reveal spoilers (and pretty significant spoilers, at that) in the post credits scene of another movie. One the one hand, for at least some in the viewing audience, there was badness associated with the revealing of information. Anyone who saw *Ant-Man and the Wasp* first, upon going to *Avengers: Infinity War* would, well before the end of the movie, know

---

of a book series (for example, *Silence of the Lambs*), and their doing so has the effect of spoiling earlier books in the series (for example, *Red Dragon*).

[12] The fact that so many audience members at the showing I was at began talking about it ("OMG!!! That was from *Infinity War*") didn't help matters. Ironically, the cryptic nature of the spoilers was undermined by the fans who were shocked that the spoilers had been revealed. It's as if the evil creative overlords of the Marvel Cinematic Universe had rendered them unwitting accomplices.

that Thanos is ultimately successful, and that half of the sentient creatures in the universe are reduced to dust.

On the other hand, there is also good reason for thinking that they were not wrong to do so. This is because the stories of the Marvel Cinematic Universe are all related to one another. Their storylines are all connected at a number of points, the characters (and actors) make appearances in movies that are not primarily about them, the timing of the events of each movie is co-ordinated, so that every storyline works in concert with every other storyline. In this way, we can think of the events of each as all being part of one big production. Just like the separate episodes of a television series, are all just part of one big show. I'm inclined to think they were not wrong to do so, as these are their stories to tell and they can dole out the information in them as they wish, but, as was stated, these are tricky cases.

Varying Degrees of Badness and Wrongness

We've discussed cases in which it is wrong to spoil, cases in which it is not wrong to spoil, and some pretty tricky cases, where it is not entirely clear whether it is wrong to spoil (or the answer may depend more greatly on the details of the circumstances). We've not, however, discussed just how wrong it is to reveal spoilers in cases where it is deemed wrong to spoil.

Not all spoilers are created equal. For example, it would be a very bad thing, if I were to get ahold of the script for the final episode of *Game of Thrones* and post on social media which character eventually winds up on the Iron Throne. It would also be bad, but not as bad, if I were to reveal that some particular minor character died in the final episode. Both would be spoilers, but the wrongness of the first one far surpasses the wrongness of the second. People's reactions upon hearing these things would certainly bear this out. In the first case, most fans of the show would be furious, and in the second case most fans of the show would be annoyed or perturbed.

So, what accounts for the difference in the degree of wrongness? There are a number of factors that may be relevant. The extent to which a particular revealing of a spoiler is wrong is partially a function of the quantity of badness that results from the spoiler being revealed. This can cash out in a number of ways. When Cassandra posts her *The Walking Dead* death notices on Facebook, hundreds of people see them. As such considerably more badness results than were she to just tell one or two persons. Consequently, her doing so is more wrong.

Another determinant of the amount of badness that results from a spoiling is the significance of what is spoiled. This is what is occurring in the *Game of Thrones* example. Revealing the death of a minor character is significant, but not as significant as revealing who ultimately sits on the Iron Throne. So, within a particular work, one bit of information can be more significant than another. It can also be the case that one work can be more significant than another. For example, revealing something about *Westworld* (since by all accounts, it is a much better and more important work) is worse than revealing something about *Billions*. Revealing something about *Psycho* is worse than revealing something about *The Happytime Murders*.

Another factor in determining the badness of revealing spoilers, and by extension the wrongness, is the emotional investment that the person has in the work that is being spoiled. My sister is not a fan of the *Harry Potter* series, so even though it is something that should never be spoiled (she may get into it someday), it is not as bad if I spoil it for her, as it is if I spoil it for someone who is a fan and has a huge emotional investment in it.

The type of badness inflicted by spoiling also plays a role in determining degrees of badness and degrees of wrongness. Violations of autonomy, for example, don't generally yield as much badness, as things that result in experiential badness. Relatedly, things that yield more kinds of badness, on balance, typically yield more overall badness than things that result in fewer kinds of badness occurring. Another related factor is on whom the badness falls. If you ruin the ending of *Murder on the Orient Express* for me, then the badness I incur is likely worse than the badness the producer of the film incurs. All things being equal it's worse to spoil stories for children than it is for adults, as stories tend to play a more significant role in the lives of children (and in the development of their world views).

So, ultimately the amount of wrongness that occurs when a spoiler is revealed can vary greatly from case to case. Of course, there is an upper limit on the total badness, that probably falls well short of the badness of, say, a murder.

9
When You Should Spoil

One of the lessons of Chapter 7 is that it would be unwise to rely on any single moral theory to account for the badness and wrongness of spoiling. Had we, for instance, opted to base our moral assessment of revealing spoilers on Immanuel Kant's moral theory, we would have been led to the conclusion that it is always impermissible to reveal spoilers.

Kant's Formula of Universal Law would see spoiling as "acting on a maxim that one could not universalize without contradiction" (in other words, you wouldn't want others to reveal spoilers, so you shouldn't do it yourself). Kant's Formula of Humanity would see spoiling as "treating others as mere means to an end, and not as ends in themselves" (spoiling violates autonomy). In each case the prohibition against spoiling is universal, according to Kant's view. Of course, we learned in Chapter 8 that there are all sorts of circumstances in which spoiling is morally permissible.

So, we were right to reject any theory that holds that there is a universal prohibition on spoiling, and our doing so comports nicely with our common-sense intuitive grasp of when it is appropriate to spoil—virtually no one believes that you should never spoil. Now let's take things one step further. Are there cases in which we are not merely allowed to spoil, but, rather, are obligated to spoil?

Ticking Time Bombs and Runaway Trolleys

This would hardly be a philosophy book if it didn't have a few really absurd and far-fetched examples. Whenever possible, I like to go to with the standards. So, lets discuss a couple of classic scenarios, which have been slightly modified for our purposes.

> **Scenario 1.** Suppose that a Dr. Evil–style terrorist has planted a large active time-bomb under the city and is threatening to blow up the entire city and kill every citizen, if you do not reveal to him each spoiler on the list of things that should never be spoiled in Appendix 1 by 5:00 P.M. today. Of course, you reason with him all that you can, explaining that he is only harming himself, and so on, but in the end, he is insistent on hearing all the spoilers.[1] Are you obligated to reveal the spoilers?
>
> Undoubtedly, you are. As we've seen, revealing spoilers is bad, but the degree of badness varies from case to case, and there is certainly an upper limit to the badness, which doesn't begin to approach the badness that results from a city being blown up and all its citizens being killed.
>
> **Scenario 2.** There is a trolley speeding down the tracks and its operator has died. It cannot be stopped for several miles, but eventually it can be derailed safely. The trolley is heading towards a fork in the track. It is set to take the left fork, meaning that if nothing happens to switch the track, it will continue on to

---

[1] You might be wondering: why doesn't the Dr. Evil–style terrorist, just buy this book, and read the spoilers for himself. We have to assume that part of being *that* evil includes a general unwillingness to buy good things (such as this book!).

the left fork. Unfortunately, there are five incapacitated people on the tracks. If the trolley continues unencumbered it will run over the five incapacitated people,[2] and all five will be killed. Fortunately, near the fork in the tracks there is a switch which, if pulled, will divert the trolley down the right tracks where it will continue until it can be derailed without any harm coming to anyone. As all this is unfolding you realize that you are too far from the switch to get there in time to divert the trolley, but there is a man standing there. You shout "Pull the switch! People are going to die if you don't." He replies "I'm reading *Harry Potter* at the moment, tell me what becomes of Dumbledore or I won't pull the switch."[3]

As was the case with Scenario 1, whatever prohibition exists against revealing that Snape eventually kills Dumbledore (but, as is revealed later, does so at Dumbledore's request), is outweighed by your obligation to not let the five incapacitated persons on the left track die. So not only is it okay, in this case to reveal a spoiler, you are morally obligated to do so.

Okay, these are some pretty far-fetched examples (but, again, staples of moral philosophy!), though they are not without their philosophical value. What they demonstrate is that the relatively low level of badness of revealing spoilers can be justified and even be obligated when the alternative is to allow greater amounts of badness to

---

[2] When I discuss trolley cases with my students they always wonder why there are incapacitated people on the tracks. If they are there as a result of their own bad actions (for instance, they drank too much, or some such), many students have the intuition that they partially deserve their fate. I don't share this intuition, but just to avoid this sort of concern, let's suppose that the evil terrorist from the previous example drugged them and left them there.

[3] Even though this is, by design, a far-fetched case, I like to make things as plausible as possible. So, what could possibly explain the strange request from the guy at the switch? It's the brute fact that *Harry Potter* fans can be a tad weird at times.

occur. By extension, if any greater wrong is to be avoided by revealing a spoiler, then it is no longer wrong to reveal that spoiler. At least not in these sorts of cases—cases in which the discrepancy between the degree of badness of spoiling is far outweighed by the degree of badness of not spoiling.

As the cases being contrasted become closer in terms of the badness that will result, other moral factors become increasingly likely to play a significant role. As long, however, as the case can be made that by spoiling something, some other significant badness can be avoided, then one will be justified (and quite possibly even obligated) to reveal a spoiler.

At the risk of jinxing things terribly, it seems unlikely that either scenario will ever occur, so let's turn our attention to some more plausible situations in which spoiling might be obligatory.

Times When Revealing Spoilers Is Necessary

Suppose that you have a friend who is going to see *The Revenant*, which, of course, features some pretty graphic scenes in which animals are killed (including a particularly gruesome killing of a grizzly bear with a knife). Also suppose that your friend is someone that you know would not enjoy the experience of seeing this (he is on record saying that he never goes to movies that portray animal death or injury), but your friend is not aware that this occurs in the film. Since the bear attack scene in *The Revenant* is one of the most significant scenes in the film, it certainly rises to the level of spoiler.[4] Are you obligated

---

[4] *The Revenant* is not one of those movies that make the list of things that can never be spoiled, in part because it is not *that* great (but close!), and in part because the significant events of the movie are historical events, and knowledge of them is pretty much out there. So, to get this example to work, just assume that it all takes place when the film was still in the theaters on its initial run.

to tell your friend that it contains explicit graphic violence to animals? Under the circumstances as described, the answer is yes.

Your obligation to tell him about the graphic violence to animals in the movie arises because of the badness that he would incur were he to experience the film. Your obligation rests on the assumption that telling him would 1. prevent him from seeing the movie, and 2. the badness that he avoided (the bad experience of seeing the graphic violence) outweighs his having a desire frustrated, his autonomy disregarded, and his being deprived of seeing the film without having any significant advance information. Of course, you must be pretty certain that your friend will be glad that you told him. If it's a pretty close call, you should err on the side of not revealing the information.

In the case under consideration, one is obligated to spoil something for someone because one knows that the person for whom the work gets spoiled wouldn't enjoy seeing the movie because of features that the spoiler reveals. Similarly, suppose that you know someone who really hates happy endings. You may have to spoil an ending for that person so that they will avoid seeing a particular film (your spoiler might be pretty vague—"Don't go! It has a happy ending"—but as we've seen, vague spoilers can still be legitimate spoilers). There are lots of things that people react to in works of entertainment, such that they wouldn't see the movie or read the book, if they knew that it contained one of those things. For example, someone might avoid watching something that has a lot of blue language or contains nudity. It should be noted that revealing this information does not always involve revealing spoilers. For example, I was recently recommending the series *Black Mirror* to a relative. She has a pretty high tolerance for a lot of things, but absolutely cannot abide watching uncomfortable or highly visual sexual situations. So, I simply warned her to not watch the first episode of Season 1 (the one where the Prime Minister is forced to engage in intimate relations with a pig to save the life of a member of the royal family). Telling her "Don't watch the first episode; it has some sexual content that you won't like" was enough to keep her from watching, and it didn't reveal a spoiler. The moral here is that one should avoid revealing the spoiler if at all possible, so if one is obligated to convey certain information to someone, and one can do so without revealing a spoiler, one should, in fact, do so— our obligation to spoil in cases such as these is a pretty rare obligation.

In addition to cases in which you may be obligated to spoil something for someone because you know that the work contains something that the person would not want to see or read, there are cases in which one might be obligated to reveal a spoiler to someone because the work is something that they should not encounter (regardless of whether they desire to see it). There are also more controversial cases in which spoilers are revealed because the person or group doing the spoiling does not want people to see the work in question, which is a distinct issue from whether it is something that the person should not see, although sometimes the person or group doing the mass spoiling doesn't see it that way. We will address these types of cases in the next section.

There could be any number of reasons why someone should not see or read a particular work. Perhaps the least controversial cases of this type are ones where one could reasonably be assured that their doing so would likely result in some badness (distinct from the badness described above where the person, if they hadn't received the spoiler, just wouldn't enjoy the film or show, etc.). Consider, for example, the case of someone who suffers from pretty severe PTSD from having served in the armed forces during wartime, and who is about to go see a movie that is about war, but they don't realize that it is that type of film. I suspect that in the 1970s a fair number of Vietnam War veterans wandered into *The Deer Hunter* without realizing just how intense what they were about to see really was. This is just one type of case where a film might have a triggering effect. Suppose that someone who has recently lost a young child and is having a demonstrably difficult time (who wouldn't?) is about to go see *A Quiet Place* in which a young child is killed in the very first scenes. Under this circumstance one may be obligated to reveal that spoiler for him or her. Of course, if there is a way to warn the person in question without revealing the spoiler, then one ought to do so, but that is not always possible.[5]

Cases of this type need not involve anything as severe as the potential triggering of one's PTSD or inducement of a panic attack. They can just be cases in which it is demonstrable that encountering some work will induce some sort of bad experience that is beyond someone's merely not enjoying that type of work. Suppose that you know someone who gets very worked up about political or social issues and that the show he is about to watch advocates a certain political line that really pushes this guy's buttons. Under the circumstances you have an obligation to reveal a spoiler.

Another type of case might involve some more traditional instances of justified paternalism. If, for example, my thirteen-year-old son wanted to watch a particular horror film that in my opinion is perhaps a little too intense for him—I'm thinking of something like Stephen

---

[5] Spoiler warnings that are also trigger warnings can make for tough cases, as it is often the case that offering a trigger warning on a topic is, by itself, enough to trigger the very thing that the warning was designed to prevent.

King's *It* here—I might forbid him to see it. I know full well, however, that my forbidding it may not be sufficient to prevent him from watching it (kids his age tend to be pretty sneaky). Under circumstances such as these revealing to him the nature of the intensity (telling him that a girl about his age is assaulted by her father and a creepy clown does really cruel things to little kids) may be sufficient to prevent him from going to see it, in a way that merely telling him that it is intense may not. One could easily imagine similar cases in which revealing information about the content of a work to a person whose religious or moral beliefs prevent them from seeing certain kinds of content might also create an obligation to reveal spoilers.

Spoiling as Social Protest

In Chapter 1 we discussed Roger Ebert's now legendary column in which he argued that critics do not have the right to reveal spoilers. His article was addressed to film critics, but it was motivated by, and in direct response to, conservative columnists Rush Limbaugh and Michael Medved, who revealed the ending of the film *Million Dollar Baby* primarily because they objected to its positive stance toward voluntary active euthanasia. This, however, was not the first time that spoilers were revealed for political reasons. In 1992 a number of gay rights groups revealed who the killer was in the film *Basic Instinct* by posting flyers that said "Catherine did it." They also drove by theaters across the county just prior to the movie's start times shouting that Catherine was the killer (in some cases they marched with spoiler-revealing picket signs in front of the theaters). Their actions were a means of protesting the way that lesbian and bisexual women were portrayed in the movie (and in movies in general).

These activities raise the question of whether it is morally acceptable, and perhaps even morally required, to reveal spoilers for political reasons.

Let's look at each of these cases in turn. The motivation for revealing the ending of *Million Dollar Baby* had to do with Limbaugh's and Medved's rejection of a view on euthanasia that gets advocated in the film. Their actions can be seen as a move in their overarching plan to ultimately win the culture wars (which by the way are still ongoing, with little hope of resolution in sight). It is worth noting that many conservatives, such as Limbaugh and Medved, consider euthanasia to be unethical, but this is a topic on which there is little consensus. Euthanasia is a controversial topic that at the time was (and still is) being widely debated. If their goal was to raise awareness of the issue, given how widely discussed it already was at the time, their actions were unlikely to achieve the goal. Moreover, raising awareness of the issue by behaving in what is by all accounts petty behavior, is more likely to push people away from their position. (Limbaugh and Medved came off looking like real jerks, especially after Ebert took them to task for it.) If their goal was to reveal spoilers in order convince people that euthanasia was wrong, given that they weren't providing anything like evidence or arguments for their position, their actions did nothing to achieve that goal, either. It seems like they just wanted to punish those who believe differently from them, and perhaps reinforce their conservative *bona fides* with their listening audiences. In sum, this was mostly just grandstanding.

Regarding the moral permissibility of their actions, it seems like their revealing spoilers was wrong for a number of reasons. First, people were harmed in all the ways that having something spoiled can be harmed—people who purchased tickets didn't get to see the movie unspoiled (desires were frustrated, autonomy was violated, people were deprived of things). Second, to the extent that Limbaugh and Medved were attempting to punish the makers of *Million Dollar Baby* (Clint Eastwood and company), they were attempting to do so without having any proper authority to punish. People have the right to stand up against injustice, but making a movie favoring euthanasia is not unjust (even if euthanasia turns out to be unjust).[6] So while it may be okay to protest and speak about the content of a movie that you don't like or that you find morally objectionable, that doesn't give you the right to spoil that movie for potentially thousands of movie-goers.

Third, the net result of their actions can be seen as a spoiling (in some sense) of someone else's artwork. This is the sort of thing that should not ever be done lightly (if ever!). Finally, it's relevant that the thing that they are objecting to on moral grounds is somewhat controversial. Things *might* be different if the message being promoted in the film is one that most people on all sides found objectionable (for example, a movie that advocates reinstating slavery). Since euthanasia is a topic on which reasonable people might disagree, the taking of such drastic actions exhibits a disrespect for their fellow citizens that is unwarranted.

In the *Basic Instinct* case things are somewhat different. The motivation for revealing that Catherine was the killer was to stop an ongoing injustice: the stereotypical portrayal of lesbians and bisexual women in cinema as evil, dangerous, unable to control their sexual desires, and violent. Unlike the *Million Dollar Baby* case, their motivations weren't to punish the film-makers. This is not an

---

[6] To be clear, I'm not suggesting that euthanasia is unjust. I'm just willing to grant it for the sake of making this point.

issue on which most people disagree. Most people are (and those who are not certainly should be) opposed to stereotyping and perpetuating only negative images of members of a particular group. Moreover, these protests brought attention to those issues, and in response to protests such as these, Hollywood has changed somewhat. So, the groups involved in the protests can be seen as acting for the right reasons.

Does that justify spoiling? Unfortunately, for them, it does not. There are still the problems of the harms to innocents and of spoiling the artwork of others. Perhaps if significant social change had come about as a result of the spoiling of *Basic Instinct* and the spoiling was necessary, then, given the altruistic motivations for the spoiling, it would be morally permissible, and, perhaps, it would even constitute a moral obligation on the part of the protesters. This particular form of protest, however, was not necessary. For the most part, it was just a stunt. The episode of *Buffy the Vampire Slayer* in which Tara was killed led to similar protests over the treatment of lesbian characters in television programs. These protests were well-co-ordinated and loud, and drew considerably more attention to the issue than did the *Basic Instinct* protests, and, most importantly for our purposes, did so without revealing spoilers. Activists would be better served finding other means by which to promote their issues.

10
The Timing of Spoilers

There's no shortage of opinions on social media about *when* things can and cannot be spoiled. A quick Google search for "spoiler etiquette" brings up a slew of articles telling both where and when things can be spoiled.

What most of these articles have in common is that the positions they are endorsing are not particularly well thought out or well argued for. In fact, there are a number of articles that make reference to the fact that the author has given "just a few minutes" thought to the issues.[1] In some cases the rationales provided for the proposed spoiler time lines amount to little more than pithy one-liners, such as "If you care enough about a show to be upset at its being spoiled, you should not be waiting a year to watch it."[2] That might sound good at first glance, but there could be any number of reasons why someone might wait a long time to watch a show or movie, which have nothing to do with how much or little they care about it.

---

[1] See, for example,
<https://www.broadbandchoices.co.uk/blog/spoiler-etiquette-how-not-to-be-a-total-joffrey>.
[2] <http://www.vulture.com/2008/03/spoilers_the_official_vulture.html>.

Another thing that many of these articles have in common is an overly simplistic approach taken in determining when it's okay to spoil something. Typically, what we find is a list of types of things that can be spoiled (for example, sporting events, movies, or television shows) and a corresponding spoiler expiration date (for example, immediately, one year after the release of the DVD, or one week after it has aired). In some cases, the accounts focus on the means by which the spoiling occurs (for instance on social media or around the water cooler at work), but fail to make much reference to the type of work being spoiled. The situation is much more complicated than this. In addition to the different rules for the various types of works of entertainment, there are different rules for the various means of revealing spoilers (in person versus on social media), and across social media platforms there are different rules that apply (for example, some social media platforms are fandom-specific, and may have generally accepted rules that supersede the general societal rules for when spoiling is acceptable).

One thing of note about these various spoiler etiquette guides is that there is not much consensus over when spoilers can be revealed. Opinions differ greatly. Moreover, in one online survey there were some pretty shocking results that that did not jibe with what the author of the article expected, nor with what people tend to proffer about the timing of spoilers in casual conversation.[3] What this means for our purposes is that our desired reflective equi-

---

[3] In May 2016 *Vulture* conducted an online poll regarding the timing of revealing spoilers. While this survey was not scientific, it did have a large number of respondents (over 2,200). Around a quarter of the respondents thought that movie and television plot points could be spoiled right away and about another quarter thought that these things could be spoiled within a few days. The results can be viewed here:
<http://www.vulture.com/2016/05/presenting-the-results-of-vultures-spoiler-poll.html>.

librium between our theoretical account of spoilers and people's intuitions regarding spoilers will not apply to the timing of spoilers in the way that it does regarding both the metaphysics of spoilers and the badness of spoilers. There can't be a similar match between the theoretical and the people's intuitions, as there is simply no consensus of intuitions regarding the timing of spoilers. So, what is called for in this situation is an account of when it is acceptable to reveal spoilers (under the various complex circumstances described above) that is based, at least to the extent possible, on those features of our account of both the metaphysics and ethics of spoilers that are in reflective equilibrium with our commonsense intuitions regarding spoiling. Such an account should have broad appeal to those whose intuitions regarding the timing of spoilers may differ from what our account prescribes.

General Rules for Revealing Spoilers

Since there are a number of factors that determine when a spoiler can be revealed, let's begin with a general account—one that does not take into consideration particular circumstances, such as whether the reveal is occurring on social media and where on social media the reveal is occurring. We can add those nuances and distinctions a little bit later in the chapter. Perhaps it is best to view these rules as being general rules for not revealing things directly to friends, family, co-workers, and people at parties or other social functions.

This might be a good time to remind ourselves that while our account primarily pertains to impersonal spoilers, a good practice is to never reveal personal spoilers, unless, of course, one of the special circumstances detailed in the previous chapter arises (for example, a ticking time bomb that threatens an entire city will be set off, if a particular personal spoiled is not revealed). Again, the idea is to avoid being a jerk whenever possible.

Significant changes in how we engage works of art has served to affect when spoilers expire. For example, it is now easy to binge-watch television programs, whereas not too long ago it was somewhat difficult to watch things other than when they first aired (or possibly during the summer re-run season). Our movie-watching habits have also changed, as our options for watching movies has increased. Previously, we could only watch movies while the films were in the theater or several years later when (in some but not all cases) they aired on television. The ability to rent movies on video tape improved the situation somewhat, but we were still pretty much limited to watching rentals when we were in close proximity to a VHS player (or a Sony Betamax player, if we guessed incorrectly which technology was destined to prevail).

DVD and Blu-ray players improved the production quality of what we consumed (if you haven't watched something on VHS, you may want to do so, if only to laugh at what previous generations had to endure), but only slightly increased our viewing options. Now, of course, we have streaming and digital downloads, which allow us to watch movies and television programs at our leisure almost anywhere we desire. Even our reading options have changed. Prior to the advent of digital book readers such as Kindle, you would have to carry any book along with you that you planned to read. This served to restrict the number of books you had access to at any particular time, except, perhaps, when you were at home or at a library.[4]

---

[4] For those of you who have never set foot in, or even heard of, a library, these were wonderful places where you could gain access to a variety of books on all sorts of topics. They were also quiet places, so it was really easy to read there.

Now anyone with a smartphone literally has access to millions of titles at virtually any time.

You might expect that having all these options for engaging works of entertainment would decrease the amount of time it takes for a spoiler to expire. The thought being that you have a responsibility to view or read something within a reasonable period of time, and given that your options for doing so have increased, then what constitutes a reasonable period of time must have shortened. This would likely be correct, if it were not for the fact that at the same time, the number of books, television programs, and movies has also increased, and not proportionately. We now have, at our fingertips, access to nearly every work of entertainment ever created (live theater and live musical performances would, of course, count as counterexamples to this). And considerably more works are being created than at any point in the past. Up until relatively recently only the three networks (ABC, CBS, and NBC) produced original programming for television. Now we have a number of other networks creating shows, along with cable networks, such as HBO and Showtime, and basic cable networks such as FX, TBS and AMC, and streaming services such as Netflix, Amazon, and Hulu (and many others!).

Similarly, there are more movies being released at any given time than were being released previously. The same goes for books, comic books, and graphic novels (especially with self-publishing options). The sheer volume of things that we may be interested in engaging is relevant. People have to be more strategic about how and when they engage works of entertainment in order to make sure that they don't miss things they prefer not to miss, or fall too far behind. In general, people plan what they're going to watch or read, and the phenomenon of planning has had the effect of often delaying when entertainment gets consumed. An account of what counts as a reasonable time for people to have viewed or read something must be sensitive to people's actual practices, provided that the actual practices are reasonable. The payoff is that people are taking longer on average to engage particular works of entertainment, and, as a consequence, spoiler shelf lives are expanding, not contracting.

Recall that our reason for not just simply maintaining that we should never spoil anything (in other words, our reason for maintaining that spoilers never expire) is that we need to balance our respect for the viewing experiences of others with a desire to discuss things that are important to us with friends, family, and co-workers. The very reasons that spoilers get us so worked up is the fact that the shows, books, and movies play an important role in our lives. Occasionally, you will hear someone say that they don't mind spoilers. In my experience, this is typically someone who doesn't have much of an emotional investment in whatever it is that might be spoiled for them. So, our question is how we strike a balance between these two competing concerns, each of which seems quite reasonable.

Let's begin with television programs. One early Internet guide put the expiration date of television program spoilers (for regular, narrative television shows such as dramas or situation comedies) at one day after the initial airing.[5] While streaming options were limited in 2008, when the article initially appeared, today that would not be considered a reasonable amount of time. It may have been reasonable then because once the show had aired, very few would have had a later opportunity to view it until it appeared in re-runs or came out on video (pretty much only the select few who had DVRs or VCRs fell into

---

[5] <http://www.vulture.com/2008/03/spoilers_the_official_vulture.html>.

this category, and a large percentage of the VCR set didn't know how to set their recorders). Since the segment of the public that was seeing particular shows for the first time when they were released on video or while being rebroadcast was a very small percentage of the viewers, a day after the initial airing was a reasonable amount time to wait to reveal spoilers (this allowed for the show to air in all time zones).

In short, by that time most people who were going to see a program had already seen it. If this were the standard that we were going to employ today, we might tighten it up so that the spoilers expired immediately after the show aired in the westernmost time zone in which it is going to air (or after the latest international airing). One thing to note about this account is that it turns out to be somewhat difficult to spoil television shows. You could, for example, reveal something you had just seen to someone in a later time zone, or, perhaps you could reveal something you heard in advance was going to happen in a particular episode, but that's about it. Opportunities to spoil under this time frame were somewhat sparse. This is where our desired reflective equilibrium comes into play. Our intuitions tell us that if I reveal to someone who is waiting to watch *American Horror Story: Apocalypse* until it is released on Netflix that in the second episode Rubberman from *American Horror Story: Murder House* makes an appearance, then I've revealed a legitimate spoiler, and that my doing so is not reasonable. Alternatively, if someone said that they were waiting until the entire series was over to watch all of it, then my reveal wouldn't count as a legitimate spoiler, as that is much too long to reasonably expect people to wait to discuss it (although it may count as a personal spoiler, under the right circumstances).

Regarding typical television programs (meaning narrative programming on networks, basic cable, and premium cable), it is impermissible to reveal any spoilers until they have been released on each of the main streaming sources that are going to be releasing them (excluding those sources that may not initially opt to stream a particular program, but may decide to do so well into the future). The circumstances vary greatly depending on both the particular program and which network the show originally airs on. *American Horror Story*, for example, typically airs in the fall. A season that airs in 2018 will likely arrive on Netflix about twelve months later, but will not arrive on Amazon or Hulu for about thirteen months (based on recent history). So, the earliest that it would be acceptable to reveal spoilers for this particular show is thirteen months. But even that would be too soon. People need an opportunity to watch the shows, and can't be expected to binge watch them the day that they are streamed (although, that is not an uncommon occurrence). It strikes me as reasonable to give people the same amount of time they would have had to watch a series, had they watched it when it first aired. So, in the case of *American Horror Story* spoilers from the 2017 season, which began airing in September of 2017, expire twelve weeks (one week per episode) after their October 2018 release date on Amazon or Hulu, whichever is later.

We can contrast this with television programs that are created for streaming services, such as *The Handmaid's Tale*, which is a Hulu original program. With programs such as *The Handmaid's Tale* the episodes are released all at once. In these cases, there is no significant lag time between the show's initial release and its arrival on the other streaming services that it will end up on (such as Amazon). As was the case with network programs, it's reasonable to give people one week per episode to watch the entire season. So, the only difference between network television programming and direct to streaming programming is in the former case we add the amount of time it takes for the program to make its way to the streaming services to the normal spoiler shelf time (one week per episode) and in the latter case we do not.

The spoiler shelf life for non-narrative television programming, such as sporting events and awards programs is considerably shorter. As was pointed out in Chapter 4, sports programming and other live event programming can legitimately be spoiled, but since this type of programming shares something in common with the news, people's interest in discussing it right away is increased. This, as we saw, creates an expectation for the person who does not watch such programming live to let those around them know that they have recorded it to watch later. In cases where this does not occur, non-narrative spoilers can be revealed right away.

The rules for when you can reveal spoilers about movies is not nearly as complicated as they are regarding television. Again, people's actual viewing practices are relevant to the question of when movie spoilers expire. Since plenty of folks wait to view movies until they can be streamed, watched on video, or watched on cable or satellite On Demand services, spoilers expire once films have been released on these services and a reasonable amount of time has passed, allowing folks time to view in a timely fashion. What counts as a reasonable amount of time? Most first-release films are in theaters for about one month. In some cases, movies that are not well received are pulled from the theaters much earlier, and in other cases, movies that are doing very well are in the theaters much longer. In the case of films that are pulled early, it's clear that people, for the most part, are not interested seeing them. In the case of movies that are in theaters longer than one month, it's safe to assume that they stay longer because people see them more than once.[6] So shortened runs and extended runs are not relevant for our purposes. It makes sense, then, to allow those who choose to view films on video, or by streaming, etc., the same amount of time as folks have to view a film in the theater. Some films are not released in the theaters; rather, they go straight to streaming or video. The same guidelines, about one month from the release date, apply to the shelf-life of these spoilers.

In general, people are not as likely to spoil books as they are movies and television programs. The main reason for this is that our desire to spoil things is not a desire to spoil things, *simpliciter*; rather, it is a desire to discuss works with people who are engaging the same things that we are (or are going to engage the same things that we are). For example, Cassandra's *The Walking Dead* death notices on Facebook are posted in a good faith effort to commiserate with friends who are also fans of *The Walking Dead*. Since at any given time, it is unlikely that your friends, family, and co-workers are reading the same novel, the desire to reveal spoilers pertaining to the novel is likely not as great. Of course, at times, there are exceptions to this. The *Harry Potter* books, the *Hunger Games* books, and (ugh!) the *Fifty Shades of Grey* books were all heavily anticipated and widely read as soon as they were released. But, generally, most books, including those on the best-seller lists, are not being read by more than a few members of any given social circle, at any particular time. This is not to suggest that people don't reveal spoilers about books, nor is it meant to suggest that it's okay to reveal spoilers about books. Rather, it just means that the rules for revealing spoilers will need to take these things into account.

---

[6] *E.T.* was in the theaters for over one year.

For the most part novels are not considered timely in the way that movies and television programs are. By design, a novel, if good, will be as enjoyable now as it was in the past and will be in the future. Television programs and movies, by contrast, can seem pretty dated in fairly short order. Television programs from the 1950s and 1960s that at the time seemed very modern, such as *The Twilight Zone* and *Star Trek* now seem extremely dated (laughably so, in the case of *Star Trek*, with its computers that don't look as sophisticated as the one this book is being written on). People might still love these programs and deem them good, but, at least part of their goodness, now lies in their kitsch value. Many programs from the 1960s that people considered great do not stand the test of time. *The Real McCoys* and *The Adventures of Ozzie and Harriet*, for example, both seem kind of hokey in a way that is neither kitschy nor cool. This fact about novels—that the goodness of novels is not timely in the same way that books and movies are—serves to extend their spoiler shelf-life. People don't have the same pressing need to read something right when it comes out (the *Harry Potter*, *Hunger Games*, *Fifty Shades of Grey* examples notwithstanding). One year after a book's release seems like a reasonable amount of time to allow someone to read a novel, prior to discussing it. Since one's desire to discuss books does not seem to be as strong as one's desire to discuss television programs and films, it's acceptable to ask folks to wait a bit longer. An exception to this would be books that are still on the best-seller lists. Any time a book is on a best-seller list, it means that people are still purchasing the book in good numbers, which, in turn, means that there are plenty of people who are still likely to read it. So, a book's spoiler shelf life is either one year or the point at which it drops off the best-seller list, whichever is later.

Plays (and similar theatrical events, such as operas), like novels, also tend to be less timely, in the sense described above, than are television programs and movies. Thus, the same considerations apply to plays, etc. as applied to novels. There is one exception: successful plays typically have a run on something like Broadway or London's West End theater district followed by touring companies appearing in large cities. This process takes a pretty long time to play out (sometimes several years), as many people are interested in seeing plays, but are willing to wait to see them until they arrive in their town. For plays of this type (big and popular Broadway productions) it's reasonable to expect people to wait until the touring companies have finished at least one tour around the country (this applies to all countries that will feature touring company versions of the play around the time of its first major run on Broadway, the West End, or the like). For plays that don't make it to Broadway or the West End, then their spoiler shelf-life extends to the end of their first run, wherever that may be.

Notice that the above account jibes nicely with our intuitions regarding both the metaphysics of spoiling and the badness of spoiling, in that it holds that spoilers have reasonably short shelf lives, that we should respect people's actual viewing practices, and that there is value to being able to discuss works of entertainment that we find interesting or compelling without having to wait too terribly long to do so. So, even though people's intuitions about how long we should have to wait to reveal spoilers can vary greatly, that doesn't bear on our ability to produce an account of when spoilers expire that comports nicely with our more fundamental intuitions regarding the revealing of spoilers.

Social Media and Spoiler Shelf Lives

What about spoilers and social media? By and large, the expiration dates of spoilers revealed on social media are the same as described above. As the Cassandra example serves to illustrate, not everyone got that memo. Still, there exist some critical differences and some subtle nuances between the rules for spoiling on social media and the rules for revealing spoilers in general.

One popular misconception is that it is okay to post vague spoilers on social media prior to a spoiler's shelf life expiring, even when it would be impermissible to directly tell someone the same vague spoiler. On multiple occasions I've witnessed someone posting a vague spoiler on Facebook, followed by a swift admonishment not to spoil from someone else, which is met with a retort to the effect that it is okay to post vague spoilers. As we've seen, vague spoilers are still spoilers and can lead to just as much badness as non-vague spoilers, and, hence, should not be treated differently.

Another popular misconception is that the shelf-life of spoilers on social media is considerably shorter. Some advocate for a two-day ban on spoilers on Facebook and Instagram, after which time "anything goes."[7] While some certainly have adopted this practice (some jerks don't even wait two days!), there is no rationale for thinking this is right. If we tie the expiration date of spoilers to the badness of spoiling (as balanced against our reasonable desire to want to discuss interesting bits of pop culture with others who have common interests), we see that, *prima facie*, the rules for social media sites should be comparable to the general rules for spoilers. Whatever speaks against revealing spoilers in general also speaks against

---

[7] <https://www.makeuseof.com/tag/okay-post-spoilers-social-media>.

revealing spoilers on social media. In fact, while the shelf life for spoilers on social media is approximately the same as it is in general (we'll get to the differences shortly), there is good reason for individuals to wait even longer to reveal spoilers on social media. Given that most people on social media have lots of friends on Facebook or tons of followers on Instagram or Twitter (ranging from the hundreds to the tens of thousands), the potential that any particular sharing of a fact about a work of entertainment has to reveal a personal spoiler is so great, that you ought to err on the side of caution well beyond the expiration date of that spoiler. It's simply the decent thing to do.

Someone might object that part of the point of social media is to connect people so that they can discuss things such as spoilers with friends (or groups of friends) who cannot all be in the same place or on the same phone call as well as with complete strangers, acquaintances, and members of fandoms that you're in. In other words, both the desire and need to discuss spoilers in a social media forum might be greater than our normal desire and need to discuss spoilers (it's really fun to discuss things on social media), such that we need to strike a different balance between our obligation to not reveal spoilers and our desire to discuss works, with the result being that on social media the spoiler shelf life is considerably shorter. I'm quite sympathetic to this line of thought, but there is a response that I find equally compelling: we can have it both ways! It is possible to respect people's right not to have things spoiled while simultaneously accommodating people's desire to discuss things on social media sooner rather than later.

First, we can simply issue a spoiler alert prior to revealing a spoiler. We will discuss spoiler alerts in greater detail in Chapter 11, but as long as you issue a spoiler alert and take the steps necessary to conceal the spoiler, you can put out whatever spoilers you like. Second, there are venues on social media where the rules for posting spoilers are different. This occurs by stipulation. On certain fan sites, such as the FanX Facebook discussion page, at least in the case of major releases, such as a Marvel Cinematic Universe or *Star Wars* offering, no one gets offended when a spoiler is revealed more than seven days after the opening.

There are other venues which designate themselves to be spoiler sites, where spoilers can be freely discussed at any time without having to issue spoiler warnings or scroll down a good while to see each comment. Since everyone on the site knows that it's a place where spoilers are discussed, no one gets any information that they don't desire to receive (it's as if the entire site functions as a properly issued spoiler alert). Of course, it is impossible to delineate specific rules for sites that have different rules regarding spoilers or even to specify what distinguishes sites where spoilers can be revealed early from those where the regular rules for revealing spoilers are not applicable, but there is an easy fix for that, too. Simply, ask the people posting on the site what the site policies are. Generally, you will get a clear answer. If you do not, then assume that the regular rules apply.

11

The Ethics of Spoiler Alerts

Thus far we have been speaking about the general prohibition against revealing spoilers, in mostly absolute terms. Of course, there have been exceptions, and these exceptions have involved cases in which either the spoiler has expired, or the spoiler occurs in an acceptable context, such as in a movie trailer, or involves cases in which revealing the spoiler will save someone from some potentially greater harm, such as seeing something triggering, and so forth.

The exceptions to the general prohibition are fairly uncommon (except in the case of movie trailers, which, as we have seen, are easily avoided). Speaking of spoilers in mostly absolute terms, however, is somewhat misleading, as lurking behind the scenes the whole time has been the ubiquitous spoiler alert—a sort of "get out of jail free card" for would be spoiler revealers. While spoiler alerts are issued frequently nowadays, they are not always used in the right way, and they are somewhat more complicated in their mechanics than they initially appear.

Speech Acts and Spoiler Alerts

So, just what are spoiler alerts? At the most fundamental level they are a warning that a spoiler is forthcoming, which is why they are sometimes called "spoiler warnings." Or, at least, ideally this is the case—sometimes what follows a spoiler alert is something that is not a legitimate spoiler or not even a spoiler at all. But there is more to the picture than that. To see why, consider some typical (non-spoiler) warnings. A particular road sign, for example, may warn a driver that she is in an area where deer frequently cross the road. A payment due notice may warn someone that they will be assessed a penalty if their payment is not received by such and such a date. A student progress report might inform a parent that her child will not receive a passing grade for a particular class, if the child's performance does not improve. What each of these examples has in common is that the warning given does not do much more than that—they merely issue warnings. The deer crossing sign, for example, doesn't do much beyond warning drivers about a potential road hazard. The same is true for the other examples. This is not the case, however, with spoiler alerts.

Like the warnings we've just considered, spoiler alerts issue a standard warning, in this case that a spoiler is about to be revealed, but spoiler alerts serve a further function, as well. The spoiler alert (if properly executed) serves to make it acceptable to reveal the spoiler. It renders the revealing of the spoiler morally permissible, and it shifts the responsibility for any badness that results from the spoiler being revealed from the person who reveals the spoiler to the person who hears or reads the spoiler.

Philosophers and linguists who work on what is called "Speech Act Theory" discuss performative utterances. A performative utterance is a sentence that in addition to conveying information of some sort or other, also has the function of making something the case that was not previously the case (it literally alters reality in some way). A promise is a good example of a performative utterance. If I say to my wife "I promise to mow the lawn," then, in addition to informing her that I will be mowing the lawn, I've also obligated myself to mow the lawn. Reality has changed upon my making a promise, as something exists (my promise to mow the lawn) which did not exist previously.[1]

If while acting in my capacity as an ordained-over-the-Internet wedding officiant I say to the groom and bride "I now pronounce you husband and wife," my doing so actually makes it official that they are married. Again, reality has changed—a couple that was not married is now married, the number of married people has increased, and the number of single people has decreased. There are a great many types of performative utterances: swearing or oath taking, certain commands, telling someone that they are hired or fired, promising, guaranteeing, proclamations, christening or baptizing, and so on. Properly issued spoiler alerts are also performative utterances.

Spoiler alerts, however, constitute a unique type of performative utterance, in that there is not the same direct connection between what is uttered and what is made the case as we see in the previous examples. For instance, my uttering the words "I promise" creates a promise, and my uttering the words "I now pronounce you husband and wife" makes it official that some happy couple is, in fact, husband and wife. Similarly, if I strike my boat with a bottle of champagne and say "I christen you 'The Spoiler Alert'," then my doing so makes it the case that it is now and forever known as "The Spoiler

---

[1] It's not the case that every such utterance is a performative utterance; rather, only the first instance is. If I say on Monday that "I promise to mow the lawn on Saturday" then my utterance is a performative utterance. If I say it again on Tuesday, since I've not created a new promise (I've just reiterated an old one), it's not a performative utterance.

Alert."[2] When you issue a spoiler alert your utterance has an extra effect on reality, but it is an effect on the ethics of revealing a spoiler, as opposed to making the spoiler alert official, in the way that christening something makes the name official. It serves, as we said, to remove the prohibition on spoiling and shift the responsibility of the badness to the person who chooses to ignore the spoiler warning, which actually denotes two shifts in reality.

The Mechanics of Spoiler Alerts

So how exactly do spoiler alerts work? If we were to pose this question to Cassandra, she would likely respond that first, you say (or write) "spoiler alert," and then you are free to immediately reveal the spoiler. On those rare occasions when she has issued a spoiler alert to me, she has always just blurted out the words "spoiler alert" and then revealed the spoiler in considerably less time than it would take for someone to stop her from spoiling whatever it is that she is attempting to spoil. Unfortunately, this has become quite common. I suspect that many people believe that the mere stating of the expression "spoiler alert" is sufficient to either make it okay to reveal a spoiler or to get them off the hook for having revealed the spoiler (sometimes people say "spoiler alert" after revealing the spoiler, as if that somehow makes it better).

Just as we tend to not place warning signs in places where it would be too late to heed the warning upon reading them (I'm imagining a sign that says "Bridge out!" placed at the far end of where the bridge would be or a sign that says "Beware of dog" on the same side of a fence

---

[2] I don't currently own a boat, but I'm assuming that once this book spends a year or two on the *New York Times* bestseller list, and subsequently is adapted into a major motion picture, I'll have enough disposable cash to purchase a modest yacht.

that the dangerous dog is on), a spoiler alert should not be given a just mere moment or two before the spoiler is revealed. A person must have at least enough time to take whatever steps are necessary to ensure that they don't hear the spoiler, if that's what they desire. They should be given enough time, for example, to say "Please don't tell me any spoilers" or to leave, or to put their fingers in their ears and begin humming loudly—whatever it takes. The same thing applies to spoilers in print. If, for example, you're planning to reveal that in *Game Night* the surprise twist is that the entire debacle is masterminded by the seemingly dim-witted neighbor, Gary, the details of the spoiler should not be visible at the same time the words "spoiler alert" first appear. All of this seems to be basic common sense, but almost everyone has encountered the spoiler that came so closely on the heels of the spoiler alert that it was impossible to avoid.

So, although the mechanics of spoiler alerts are not terribly complicated, the fact that so many people do it wrong makes the mechanics worth spelling out. The first step is to begin by giving a spoiler warning. It need not use the words "spoiler alert," but something that makes it clear that a spoiler is to follow. The second step is to reveal the spoiler in such a way as to make hearing or reading the spoiler avoidable. In this book, for example, a complete chapter by chapter list of works spoiled occurs prior to the first section.[3] A reader can determine in advance if there are any chapters they need to set aside for the time being. This is appropriate for print media, blogs, radio and television programs, podcasts, and so forth.[4] In conversation,

---

[3] If you dove right in without reading the introduction, then you got what you deserved.

[4] On our popular culture and philosophy podcast, *I Think, There I Fan*, Rachel Robison-Greene and I issue a spoiler warning at the beginning of each episode, which lists works that get spoiled during the episode. I would like to see this become standard practice.

a long pause should be sufficient (provided that the listener has a chance to react to the pause and register their desire not to hear the spoiler). On social media, you can simply put enough blank lines between the spoiler warning and the text that contains the spoiler, so as to force the reader to scroll down in order to see the revealed information. Some social media sites, such as Reddit, are now offering spoiler tags. These are tags that cover text, requiring anyone who wants to see the revealed content to click on the tag. If you're speaking in a public forum, then you should do your best to refrain from revealing spoilers, at least to the extent that it is possible, as the audience may be for all intents and purposes captive. If spoilers are not avoidable, then a warning up front is appropriate. In addition to getting the mechanics right, there is a further constraint on the content of spoiler alerts. If you reveal something that should never be spoiled, then the spoiler warning does not serve to make your doing so acceptable, nor does it shift the responsibility for the badness from the person who spoils to the person who receives the spoiler.

If a spoiler alert either reveals something that should never be spoiled or does not follow the above procedures, a misfire occurs, and the net effect is that a legitimate spoiler was revealed, just as if no spoiler warning had occurred. There are other ways in which a spoiler warning can misfire. For example, a spoiler warning can precede something that is not a legitimate spoiler, such as a piece of information that does not rise to the level of legitimate spoiler or some fact whose spoiler shelf-life has expired. In these types of cases, however, since the thing being revealed is not something that should not be spoiled, it ultimately doesn't matter that it's a misfiring. No harm, no foul, so to speak.

You might wonder why things that should never be spoiled aren't treated in the same way as other legitimate spoilers. That is, if a regular legitimate spoiler (one with a shelf-life) can be appropriately spoiled when a spoiler warning is properly employed, then why can't a spoiler that does not have a shelf-life be similarly spoiled? The problem with treating these the same is that doing so does not capture what is distinct about things that can never be spoiled, namely, their greatness. The very thing that makes it such that they can never be spoiled provides the basis for having them be such that they shouldn't be spoiled, even if a proper warning is given. These things are simply too great to spoil (again, if there is a ticking time bomb under the city, all bets are off, so to speak).

Recently, would-be spoiler revealers have taken to offering more nuanced spoiler warnings. In addition to the traditional spoiler alert we now have the vague spoiler alert, the major spoiler alert, and the minor spoiler alert. To all intents and purposes the rules for employing the nuanced spoiler alerts are pretty much the same as is the case with a traditional spoiler alert. Etiquette, of course, dictates that the type of spoiler revealed should match the type of spoiler advertised, so if the warning says "vague spoiler alert" then then spoiler should be a vague spoiler. That aside, major spoilers, minor spoilers, and vague spoilers are all spoilers, and, consequently, should be avoided. As far as I'm concerned, I don't want to hear any spoilers, but I suppose that some folks who do not want to hear non-vague major spoilers may not mind hearing minor spoilers or vague spoilers (even though vague spoilers, as we've seen, can be pretty major spoilers).

I Think We May Have a Problem Here

This book, while including the necessary spoiler warnings in the introduction, does reveal a number of things that should never be spoiled, such as that Norman Bates is

Mother and that Snape killed Dumbledore. So how do we reconcile the apparent contradiction? One way to resolve the contradiction is to hold that this book simply should not reveal such spoilers. A second possibility is to hold that revealing these spoilers is necessary for completing a book on the philosophy of spoilers. Both of these strategies seem misguided. As long as there is compelling reason to reveal spoilers of this type, the first approach fails. The second approach fails, because revealing the spoilers is not necessary. There could certainly be a book about spoilers that does not reveal any spoilers, much less spoilers that should never be spoiled.

A third strategy, which lies in between the first two, seems more promising. This possibility holds that revealing these spoilers in certain contexts is good, because of the consequences that doing so yields (much like in the case of ticking time bombs, but perhaps, not quite so extreme). To the extent that discussing certain spoilers in a book about the ethics, metaphysics, and pragmatics of spoilers serves to refine the concepts and make it explicit which things (and which types of things!) should never be spoiled, discussing spoilers under such circumstances should greatly reduce the number of spoilers that are ultimately revealed.

An analogy with the rules of *Fight Club* should help to illustrate this point. Famously, the first rule of Fight Club is that you do not talk about Fight Club (it is also the second rule). In order to tell people about the rule, you must break the rule, because telling someone the rules of Fight Club involves talking about Fight Club. Yet, it's better to talk about Fight Club a little (that is, when you're telling people the rules) than to never discuss Fight Club, because not talking about Fight Club ever would lead to an even greater number of violations of the rule.

There is a second argument that speaks in favor of books such as this one revealing spoilers that should never be revealed, even in light of a universal prohibition against revealing such spoilers. This second argument also involves an analogy. Philosophers of language, at times, will invoke what they call the "use-mention distinction." The distinction is between using a word and mentioning a word. When you use a word, you employ it in its customary way. For example, if I say "Jimmy McGill is no longer an attorney" I've *used* the word "attorney." If I say that the word "attorney" is a noun, then I've *mentioned* the word. In the first case I'm talking about an attorney, and in the second case I'm talking about the word "attorney." In the case of words that should not be used, such as slurs, the prohibition on mentioning them either does not exist or is not as strong. This is because it is sometimes valuable to discuss language, but using some words has no value (or has a sort of negative value).

Similarly, there is a distinction to be made between revealing spoilers in the customary way and talking about spoilers. By "in the customary way" I mean telling someone a spoiler for the purpose of actually spoiling that thing for them (or at least without regard for whether a spoiler gets revealed). When you spoil something that should never be spoiled, you are failing to respect the prohibition against doing so, just as in cases where someone uses a derogatory expression, even though they should not. Conversely, when you discuss things that should never be spoiled and in doing so mention one or provide an example, you're not failing to respect the prohibition against revealing spoilers; rather, you recognize that it is warranted under the circumstances, just as occasionally mentioning (as opposed to using) a derogatory slur may be warranted, provided, of course that there is actual good to be attained, and, also, provided that a spoiler warning is issued. So, it would appear that we are on solid footing in this book, after all. Whew!

When Should You Issue a Spoiler Alert?

In general, you should issue a spoiler warning whenever you're going to reveal a spoiler. There are, however, a handful of exceptions to this general rule.

If you are revealing information in a context in which it is clear that spoilers are to be revealed, and in which it is appropriate for spoilers to be revealed, then you need not issue a spoiler warning. Recall our discussion of movie trailers and television previews as spoilers. Given that, by design, they reveal spoilers, and that everyone expects the previews and trailers to reveal spoiling information, there is no need for a spoiler warning to precede the previews and coming attractions. Of course, as we have seen, there are times in which too much information is revealed, but since the audience is pretty much captive (at least in the case of the trailers being shown in movie houses), there is no point in issuing a spoiler alert; rather, the film companies should simply refrain from revealing too much information.[5]

Television content warnings can often contain spoilers. Most of the time they are sufficiently vague, so as not to reveal much of anything. They will say things such as "This program contains adult content," or "This program contains language unsuitable for children." When this occurs, no significant information is actually being revealed, so there is no need for a spoiler warning. Sometimes, however, television content warnings contain actual spoilers. They do so in the spirit of helping people make choices

---

[5] Sometimes the opposite is the case: trailers reveal so little information, that you can glean virtually nothing from the preview or trailer. With movie promotion this is pretty rare, but it is increasingly common with television programs. The producers of *Breaking Bad, Better Call Saul*, and *Mad Men* were particularly good at creating extremely cryptic previews that revealed little or nothing about the upcoming episode, but still managed to pique interest in the viewer. I'd like to see more production companies adopt this model.

that allow them to avoid being triggered, or in the spirit of helping parents decide whether the program is appropriate for children to watch, when the standard "Mature Audience" type rating doesn't provide enough information. So, on the one hand, it's a good thing that these occur. On the other hand, they will occasionally contain some pretty specific information (such as "This program graphically depicts rape). Under these circumstances a spoiler warning is appropriate.[6] This situation is different from spoilers occurring in movie trailers and television previews, because it is not commonplace. Given that television content warnings containing spoilers is rare, we don't expect them when they occur. Were they more ubiquitous, people would take steps to ensure that they didn't see them. As it is, the ones that spoil tend to blindside people.

Certain social media sites are "spoiler sites." There are a number of these on Reddit, for example. Fans of particular shows, movies, and comic books go to these sites for the express purpose of sharing spoilers, discussing spoilers, and learning spoilers. So as long as it is clear to anyone who might wander on to one of these pages, that it is a spoiler page, there is no reason to post spoiler warnings before each spoiler reveal. Not that this doesn't happen. Often people will put "Spoiler Alert!" In the title of their posts on the spoiler page. Sometimes they will even repeat the spoiler warning in the body of the post just before the reveal occurs.

Of course, when the spoiler is not a legitimate spoiler, for example, when the spoiler has exceeded its shelf life, there is no need to issue a spoiler warning. Similarly, if you have good reason to believe that the person that you're about to reveal the spoiler to already knows the

---

[6] This never occurs, but there is no reason why they couldn't lead with "The content warning you are about to see contains spoilers."

spoiler, you need not precede it with a spoiler alert. Finally, if you're in one of those situations discussed in Chapter 9 in which you find yourself obligated to spoil something, there is no need to issue a spoiler warning. If the idea is to spoil something regardless of the desires of the individual to whom the information is revealed, then issuing a spoiler warning, just serves to facilitate their avoiding the spoiler. Though these cases are rare, when they occur, feel free to spoil away!

There are certainly other circumstances in which it is okay to not give a spoiler warning. Perhaps the best policy, is to always issue one before revealing a spoiler unless you are certain that you are in one of those situations.

III

The Pragmatics of Spoilers

12
Paradoxes of Spoiling

One picture that has emerged through Parts I and II of this book is that, at least most of the time, revealing spoilers is a bad thing, and that when you do so, you've harmed others. Moreover, people can become quite upset upon having things spoiled (up to the point of stabbing their co-workers in the chest!). Given this picture, you would expect people to avoid spoilers at nearly all costs. You would also expect people to enjoy works of entertainment less, if these works have surprise twists and other spoilable features, once they have come to know those spoilable plot twists and turns. This, however, is not always the case. These facts about spoilers, along with a few others, give rise to a couple of interesting paradoxes pertaining to spoilers.

The Multiple Engagement Paradox

I very much like engaging certain works of art over and over. For example, there are books that I've enjoyed so much, such as F. Scott Fitzgerald's *The Great Gatsby*, that I revisit them every several years. The same is true for particular television programs (at the time this is being written, I am currently watching *The Office* for the second time, and *Mad Men* for the third time) and movies (the number of times that I've watched *The Princess Bride* is inconceivable!). I'm not alone in this. Most people that I know will watch or read things they like time and time again. This is not surprising. But what about those cases in which so much of the pleasure of engaging a certain work hinges on a particular spoiler? Shouldn't our experience of works such as these be diminished upon multiple viewings or readings? If it isn't, then, in what sense is anything spoiled?

Let's call this "The Multiple Engagement Paradox." People might have any number of reasons for revisiting their favorite works. For example, they might like the way the works make them feel, or they might perpetually find the comedic bits funny (some things never stop being funny), or they might enjoy the visual aspects.[1] In these sorts of cases, there is no mystery as to why someone would want to engage those works multiple times. It's not even surprising that their enjoyment on multiple engagements will not decrease, and in some cases will even increase. But with certain sorts of works, it seems reasonable to expect that enjoyment will, in fact, decrease upon subsequent viewings, once one knows the key "spoiler" or plot twist.

A paradigm case of this is the whodunit. These are stories for which a good portion of the fun is trying to figure out who perpetrated the crime before it is revealed in the story. Whodunits are fun for many of the same reasons that puzzles are fun. My favorite movie in this genre, is

---

[1] Among the things that I perpetually find funny are 1. The "I always wanted to be a dinosaur" speech from *Step Brothers*, 2. The guy in the tiger suit scene from *Monty Python's The Meaning of Life*, and 3. Clark W. Griswold's profanity-laced verbal tirade upon learning that his Christmas bonus isn't the cash he was expecting in *National Lampoon's Christmas Vacation*.

the 1974 version of Agatha Christie's novel *Murder on the Orient Express*. There are many things to love about this film, from the cinematography to the wonderful performances by Albert Finney, Lauren Bacall, and Ingrid Bergman (and others!) to the snappy dialogue, and so forth, but a large part of what is great about it is its surprise ending—that all the suspects participated in the murder. I've seen this movie approximately twenty-five times over the years, and my enjoyment hasn't diminished one iota. Herein lies our paradox. If a huge part of what I enjoyed about this film on the first viewing was the surprise ending, and on subsequent viewings my experience was not diminished in the least, then in what sense would it have been spoiled for me, had I known about the surprise ending in advance? If revealing certain information doesn't ruin anything, it seems implausible to call that reveal a spoiler. And yet, if anything counts as a spoiler, the ending of *Murder on the Orient Express* does.

Our task, then, is to give an account of works, such as *Murder on the Orient Express*, for which people's enjoyment hinges so much on a particular spoiler, and yet people's enjoyment doesn't seem to be diminished on subsequent viewings. Either we must conclude that knowing the spoiler doesn't ruin anything, which, in turn would point us away from the conclusion that spoiling is, *prima facie*, a bad thing, or we must reconcile our enjoyment of subsequent viewings or readings with the fact that some value is missing—not experiencing the twist as we did on the first viewing when we didn't see it coming—on subsequent viewings.

With certain films whose value in large part arises from a particular surprise or plot twist, there is some pleasure to be derived from multiple viewings to see all the hints we missed leading up to the twist. Three paradigm cases of this involve the surprise endings of *The*

Sixth Sense, in which Malcolm Crowe had been dead the entire time, *The Usual Suspects*, in which Verbal Kint turned out to be Keyser Söze, and *Fight Club*, in which the Narrator was also Tyler Durden. We might expect that the value that is lost in subsequent viewings (ones in which we already know the spoilable plot twist) is recaptured in those viewings by the pleasure one gains from watching with an eye toward seeing the mechanics of the twist, or looking for subtle hints that were missed the first time around, or any number of other things that come with awareness of the spoiler. This is certainly consistent with one of the conclusions of the Leavitt-Christenfeld study discussed in Chapter 6 (recall that Levitt and Christenfeld speculated that the reason that their subjects preferred the spoiled stories to the unspoiled stories may have to do with the aesthetic pleasure that comes from knowing what is coming in a story). While this appears a promising strategy for resolving the paradox, it fails to account for more than just the first few watchings. This is certainly true of my second, third, and fourth viewings of *Murder on the Orient Express*; I spent quite a bit of time just seeing how all the killers were related to one another, and wondering why I didn't "see it" the first time around.[2]

There's no denying that there is some aesthetic value to be gained from watching or reading something you've watched or read previously in order to look for critical information that you might have missed, and we have good reason to believe that such aesthetic value is at a premium in cases such as the ones currently under consideration (whodunits and stories that involve surprise endings or

---

[2] Confession time: I almost never figure out who did it when watching a whodunit, but almost always wonder how I could have missed it once it is explained. I'll admit to a certain degree of cognitive dissonance in cases like this.

unexpected plot twists). By the time I had seen *Murder on the Orient Express* two or three times, I had seen enough to tie things together—my fascination with what I had missed the first time around was over. I didn't see anything on the eighth viewing, for example, that I hadn't already seen on the fifth, sixth, and seventh viewings.

To resolve the paradox, we're going to have to look elsewhere. Let's begin by noting that it would not count as an acceptable resolution to simply deny that spoiling is bad. This is because, as we've already noted several times previously, that revealing spoilers deprives people of having certain sorts of experiences, which in and of itself is a bad thing (provided that the experience is good). So, if a spoiler gets revealed to me just prior to my watching a show I'm invested in, and my knowing the spoiler actually increases my enjoyment (I have a great time focusing on those plot points that lead to the spoiler, or some such), it is still bad that it was spoiled, because I was deprived of the experience of seeing it unspoiled.[3] Considering that after watching something unspoiled you always have the option of watching it again, the value of seeing it spoiled is still available. In short, one never gets that moment—the unspoiled watching experience—back.

So why do people like watching certain shows and movies, or reading certain books, over and over? The resolution to our paradox lies in the fact that the value of a particular work of entertainment (or more precisely, the value a particular work has for a particular consumer of that work) is not a function of the value of the individual parts (or the value that those parts have for a particular consumer). For example, the value of *Bad Times at the El*

---

[3] The various other badnesses discussed throughout Part II (desire frustration, autonomy violations, and so forth) are also applicable to this account.

Royale is not the sum of the value of Jon Hamm's portrayal of an FBI agent, plus the value of Chris Hemsworth's portrayal of a cult leader loosely based on Charles Manson, plus the value of the well-chosen soundtrack, plus the value of the set design, and so on. Instead the whole work comes together, and has a certain value. The sum is, so to speak, not equal to the aggregate value of its parts. Consequently, were one of the parts to be removed, suppose, for example, that Dakota Johnson didn't get tied up as she always does in films, the overall value would not necessarily change, nor would it necessarily change by precisely the value of the part that was removed.

In some cases, the value of the surprise ending or twist is so great that if that is removed from the equation (as is the case when one views a movie with a surprise ending multiple times) the value of the work does diminish. This is why, even though I enjoyed both *The Usual Suspects* and *The Sixth Sense* quite a bit the first time I saw them, I didn't really enjoy either on subsequent viewings. The fun of figuring out how it all happened didn't make up for the loss of the fun upon having the twist revealed the first time. This is not the case, however, with *Murder on the Orient Express*. There are so many things that are great about this movie that the loss of the value of the surprise ending doesn't even begin to put a dent into its overall value.

We see this with other films that contain significant spoilable twists and surprises. *Psycho* is perhaps the movie with the greatest surprise ever, but it's one that fans of the film can watch time and time again. Why? Because there are so many other wonderful things about the film. To be clear, had it ended differently, it would likely not be as good as it is, but it would still be the sort of movie that people want to watch more than once. The same is true of *Planet of the Apes*, *The Empire Strikes Back*, and each of the other movies that are on our list of movies that should never be spoiled. Moreover, it's not as if the great surprise is no longer part of the story once the spoiler is revealed. Part of the greatness of *Psycho* is that Norman Bates *is* Mother, which is distinct from the fact that part of the greatness of *Psycho* is that Norman Bates being Mother comes as a surprise to the audience. Similarly, that Darth Vader is Luke Skywalker's father and that the Planet of the Apes is Earth are still great parts of *The Empire Strikes Back* and *Planet of the Apes* even after the spoiler is revealed. All we've lost at that point is the surprise.

So, we see that The Multiple Engagement Paradox rests on a mistaken assumption, namely, the assumption that spoiling something entails ruining it completely or beyond enjoyment, or at a minimum diminishes the experience of engaging it to a discernable degree. This is not the case: spoiling something just ruins a part of our experience of the work.

The Westworld Rickrolling Event

On April 9th 2018 the uncontested greatest event in the history of the Internet occurred. The creators of *Westworld,* Lisa Joy and Jonathan Nolan, orchestrated what has come to be known as the "*Westworld* Rickrolling Event." While joining the Reddit community for an AMA (Ask Me Anything) session to promote Season Two of *Westworld*, Joy and Nolan made the folks of Reddit an intriguing offer. Claiming that fan theories about plot events sometimes comprise spoilers (or at least serve to blur the lines between speculation and spoiler), they offered to post a video revealing all the major spoilers of Season Two, provided that their post received a thousand upvotes.[4] This, according to Joy and Nolan would allow those who wanted to know spoilers to see them and would help clarify the

---

[4] You can view the video here: <https://youtu.be/W7oeROkyPgs>.

distinction between spoilers and speculation. Needless to say, their post had the requisite one thousand upvotes within hours. Seemingly true to their word, later that day Joy and Nolan posted a video to YouTube entitled *"West-world* Season Two—A Primer." Tens of thousands of people watched it over the next couple of days.

The video began with some scenes that had already been released in the trailers for Season Two followed by a scene in Sweetwater (the town in Westworld where visitors first arrive by train) in which Evan Rachel Wood (she plays Dolores, the heroine of sorts, in *Westworld)* sings Rick Astley's "Never Gonna Give You Up." This is followed by twenty or so minutes of a dog playing the piano. No spoilers were revealed. It was a rickrolling followed by a really obscure homage to Bento the keyboard cat.[5]

The *Westworld* Rickrolling Event is interesting for our purposes, as it raises a paradoxical question. If people have such disdain for spoilers and they go to such great lengths to avoid them, then why did over seventy thousand people flock to Joy's and Nolan's video within just a day or so of its being posted on YouTube? There exists a tension between the way people react to having things spoiled—with anger, frustration, and indignation—and the fact that fans of a show willingly attempted to learn an entire season's worth of spoilers less than two weeks before the season was to begin airing.

---

[5] Rickrolling is an unusual phenomenon in which, initially, people tried to trick others into unwittingly watching the video of Rick Astley's "Never Gonna Give You Up." Over time the concept has grown to include getting people to watch or listen to any rendition of the song (such as Evan Rachel Wood's version in the phony *Westworld* spoilers video) or to just see the words "never gonna give you up" (I recently saw a stack of books in a display arranged so the first word of each title constituted a rickrolling). A fascinating and informative discussion of the phenomenon of rickrolling can be viewed here: <https://youtu.be/xfr64zoBTAQ>.

It is worth noting that while a great number of fans of *Westworld* attempted to glean a season's worth of spoilers, there is little reason to believe that most fans of the show that were made aware of the video attempted to do so. So, the situation would be much more concerning for our account if the tension that arises in this case were a tension between how most people generally react to having something spoiled for them and the way most people would react to having the option to have a season spoiled. That said, there were quite a few people who looked at the video prior to it becoming common knowledge that it was just a rickrolling, and this needs to be accounted for.

Certainly, some of the folks who viewed the video are people who simply do not mind knowing spoilers. While there's no hard data on this, there is no reason to suppose that a very high percentage of the folks who viewed the video fall into this category, as the sample size is very large (again, over seventy thousand viewers in the first twenty-four hours), and it likely reflects society at large, where a not very large percentage of the population is agnostic about seeing spoilers. So, why would so many people who, presumably, don't like seeing spoilers, watch the video?

Part of the story has to do with weakness of the will. As we've seen people are more likely to be upset at having a spoiler revealed if they have an emotional investment in the work of entertainment. That's why the results of the Leavitt-Christenfeld study didn't match most people's attitudes about spoilers; their study involved spoilers for

---

[6] This is not to suggest that the badness of spoiling doesn't obtain in these cases. So, in that sense there are severe consequences, but they are not the sort of severe consequences you face when you spoil something for someone else—there is no admonition, no ire, no punches in the nose, no knives in the chest.

works in which people had little or no emotional invest-ment. So, it makes sense that people would be upset on learning spoilers for a show like *Westworld*, which has an extremely invested fandom. At the same time, that level of investment creates a very strong desire in its fans to know what's going to happen in the upcoming episodes. At odds in fans is a strong desire to have a quintessential viewing experience (one that is unspoiled) and a similarly strong desire to know what's going to happen right away. To avoid knowing spoilers under these circumstances really tests the will. So, part of the answer to our question is that some folks just do not pass the test. Just as some folks (even adults) will snoop to find out what they will be receiving from others for their birthday or Christmas, some people, if given the opportunity, will also snoop to find out what happens in future episodes of their favorite shows.

A second part of the story has to do with who's doing the spoiling. If my learning a spoiler has to do with my choosing to do so, I'm less likely to have a strong reaction, than if someone else revealed the spoiler. If it was my choice, I might experience a little regret, but if someone else spoils something for me, anger is the likely result. So, in the end it's not all that paradoxical that some people would willingly choose to view spoilers: from time to time temptation gets the better of all of us, and we don't face particularly severe consequences when it happens.[6]

13
Spoiling Remakes and Some Other Tricky Cases

Speaking of *Murder on the Orient Express*, in 2017 I gave a talk in Salt Lake City on the topic of spoilers. I listed what I considered to be the greatest spoilers of all time.[1] One of the things that I included on that list was the fact that in *Murder on the Orient Express* every suspect participated in the murder of John Cassetti (a.k.a. John Ratchett). The talk occurred just two months before the release of Kenneth Branagh's remake of Sydney Lumet's 1974 adaptation of Agatha Christie's 1934 novel.

As I went down the list ("Darth Vader is Luke Skywalker's father," "Norman Bates is Mother," "the Planet of the Apes is Earth," "Snape killed Dumbledore," "*To Serve Man* is a cookbook," and so on) the audience nodded in agreement and expressed no reservations about my saying these things out loud in a public forum. It was, after all, a talk on spoilers, and the appropriate spoiler warnings had been given.

When I revealed the spoiler about *Murder on the Orient Express*, however, things took a turn for the worse. I'm not going to sugarcoat it, folks: things got ugly! Someone

---

[1] See Appendix 1 for my list of the greatest spoilers of all time.

screamed "Come on!" A number of people booed. I may be misremembering things slightly, but I'm pretty sure that rotten fruit and vegetables were thrown, and some members of what had become a pretty angry mob left to find a railroad rail that they could tie me to in order to dump me in a battered heap just beyond the city limits. It was clear that they were upset that I was spoiling a movie that was about to be released.

This case raises a number of questions. Is it possible to spoil remakes? Does the existence of a remake reset the spoiler shelf-life of the original? If a movie is based on a book (or *vice versa*) can it be legitimately spoiled? Is it reasonable to expect that the remake will sufficiently resemble the original, such that it is even possible to know spoilers without having seen the remake?

Can You Spoil Remakes?

My response at the time was twofold. I said to the mob: 1. the original was released forty-three years ago, and 2. we have no compelling reason to expect that the remake would proceed along the same lines as the original. It did, of course, but no one in the room was in a position to know that.

Fortunately, that seemed to calm them down. Both of these factors are morally relevant, but the picture is more complicated than I made it seem at the time. For example, whether you have particular knowledge about the remake (beyond merely knowing that the film is being remade, and what was in the original, and so forth) is also morally relevant. Compare the following scenarios. In the first, I'm aware that a movie is being remade, but I don't know much more than that about it. Given that remakes run the gamut from being virtual copies of the original (think Gus Van Sant's frame by frame remake of *Psycho*) to being complete re-imaginings (for example, Tim Burton's 2001 version of *Planet of the Apes*, which barely resembled the original at all), attempts to reveal information about the updated version based on your knowledge of the original isn't sufficiently likely to lead to a reveal of actual information. Not that folks might not get angry with you for what they perceive to be a legitimate spoiling; it's just not a spoiling. Instead it is something analogous to telling people on their way into a murder mystery you haven't seen, that the butler did it. It may bother some who don't know that you are guessing (even if your guess is correct).

To put the matter another way, you cannot tell a secret if you don't know the secret, and if you accidentally or co-incidentally utter the secret, it still wouldn't count as an instance of telling a secret. Therefore, my telling the ending of the 1974 version of *Murder on the Orient Express* to the audience in Salt Lake City was an instance of my revealing a spoiler about the 1974 version, but not an instance of my revealing a spoiler about the 2017 version, as I had no particular information about how the latter version would end (even though it did, in fact, end as I said).

In the second scenario, I'm not only aware that a movie is being remade, but I've read that the director is going be faithful to the original plot. This sort of thing happens quite frequently. When it was revealed that Gus Van Sant was going to duplicate *Psycho* frame by frame, folks who had seen Hitchcock's version were in a position to deduce a number of facts about the remake (such as, that Milton Arbogast would get stabbed by Mother at the top of the stairs). Van Sant's approach is a bit of a novelty (to say the least), but it is not uncommon for directors to make it clear that their version is going to more closely resemble the book on which the film was based than did an earlier version. Joe Wright's 2005 version of *Pride and Prejudice* sticks considerably closer to Jane Austen's novel than does Robert Z. Leonard's 1940 version.[2] This sort of information can also allow us to determine things about the story—things which can be revealed to others. Under circumstances such as these, you can spoil remakes (as well as adaptations). Had I known that the 2017 version of *Murder on the Orient Express* was going to end the same way that the earlier version and the novel ended, when I uttered the ending, I would have been spoiling the remake. This is just one way in which remakes can be spoiled. Beyond knowing whether or not a remake is faithful (or unfaithful) to a previous version or the original source, we might know particular story lines, shooting locations, directorial intentions, and any number of other things that might constitute a legitimate spoiler.

So what bearing does the fact that remakes can be legitimately spoiled have on the spoilability of the original? In other words, does the fact that a new version exists, which can be spoiled, bear on the spoiler shelf-life of the original? While we might be tempted to think that the new version's being spoilable makes all significant information pertaining to it a potential spoiler, and this information extends back to the earlier version, I think this temptation should be resisted. The idea is that some bit of information is a legitimate spoiler, and it can hit multiple targets under circumstances in which it counts as significant information for multiple works. The very thing that makes the spoiling of remakes possible, namely, that they are works independent from the original, provides a reason for thinking that spoilers attach to works independently. Consider the aforementioned versions of *Pride and Prejudice*.[3] In both versions Elizabeth Bennet and Jane Ben-

---

[2] Although Wright's version is nowhere near as faithful to the original novel as the BBC's 1995 mini-series, which I highly recommend.

net end up with Mr. Darcy and Mr. Bingley. This is a spoiler for each version, but in the case of the 1940s version it's a spoiler whose shelf-life has long since expired, whereas in 2005 it would have been a legitimate spoiler. The single spoiler has multiple targets, but it need not attach to each target in the same way (expired in one case, and legitimate in the other). This way of interpreting spoilers that attach to multiple targets allows us to avoid the very odd result that a particular spoiler can be a legitimate spoiler for a work for a while (while the movie is in theaters and just after), cease to be a legitimate spoiler for a long period of time (over six decades in this case!), and then become one again, because of some contingent event (such as a new version of the work being produced).

But in Slasher Films the Cop Always Dies

If information based on original versions of works is not likely to lead to knowledge of what happens in remakes, since beliefs about remakes that are based on what happens in original works are not sufficiently likely to be true, then are beliefs about what will happen in particular works that are highly likely to be true, instances of knowledge about those works (and potentially legitimate spoiler material)?

Here is the sort of case that I have in mind. Suppose that you're pretty good at predicting which characters are going to get killed off in a horror film or who committed the crime in a whodunit. By this I mean, for example, that

---

[3] While it may seem natural to use *Murder on the Orient Express* as an example here, since the question under consideration arises in the context of my revealing the ending of it, the example won't quite work when discussing the spoiler shelf-life of the earlier version, as *Murder on the Orient Express* sits very near the top of the list of things that can never be spoiled.

you are able to tell about halfway through the movie who the killer is about eighty percent of the time, based on your knowledge of the genre and the tropes, mechanisms, and conceits that are typically employed. Suppose further that you are watching a movie with a friend, and in the middle, based on your recognizing certain patterns that usually play out, you correctly come to believe that the butler did it, and you whisper this to your friend. This is not an uncommon occurrence and most people do not consider this to be a spoiler. Our commonsense intuitions tell us that this is not a spoiler; rather, it is just a prediction, so ideally our account should reflect this.[4] But if reliability (or lack thereof) is the thing that distinguishes legitimate spoilers from expired spoilers in the case of remakes, then why is it not the thing that also distinguishes spoilers from non-spoilers in the case of films in similar genres?

In the case where you lacked reliability—where knowing facts about an original version was not sufficient for knowing facts about a remake—we saw that reliability was a necessary condition for having knowledge of the remake. Your method for determining what would happen in the remake was not sufficiently likely to lead to true beliefs about what was in the remake, so your method was not sufficiently reliable. A failure of reliability resulted in a failure of knowledge (even when you held beliefs that were true). Reliability's being a necessary condition for having knowledge does not, however, make it a sufficient condition. More than just mere reliability is required in this case. You also need beliefs that were produced in the

---

[4] You might be thinking "What about cases in which the likelihood that you are right is much higher?" That, it turns out, doesn't affect things. Epistemologists point out that even in lottery cases where the odds are nineteen million to one against your holding the winning ticket, you still don't know that you hold a losing ticket. It's not about the numbers, it's about the specific nature of your evidence.

right sort of way. The belief must be the result of a certain kind of epistemic virtue—one more finely attuned to true belief under the particular circumstance.

To illustrate, let's return to our example. If instead of forming your belief that the butler did it on the basis of your general knowledge of the genre and what happens in similar films, you form your belief on the basis of your putting together clues from the film in such a way that you must be right (suppose, very much to your credit, you notice exactly the same things that Hercule Poirot or Miss Jane Marple notices), then your whispering that the butler did it, would count as a spoiler—you figured out what was going to happen, and you revealed that information. This is because your belief wasn't just reliably formed, but it was reliably formed in the right sort of epistemically virtuous way—based on facts about the particular film and not just based on trends. This is what distinguishes knowledge from mere predictions (even in those cases where the prediction turns out to be true).

Spoiling for Yourself

This brings us to our second tricky case: spoiling for yourself. Suppose that in the previous case you had deduced that the butler did it, but did not whisper it to your friend. Would it be correct to say that you spoiled it for yourself? Is it even possible to spoil something for oneself?

There are at least four ways in which you might spoil something for yourself (of which only the first two are serious). The most straightforward way, and certainly the most common, is when you simply seek out a spoiler. Everyone knows someone who will get into a good book, not be able to resist the urge to see what happens, and then skip ahead to the next chapter or the last page in order to satisfy their curiosity. Similarly, people will seek out spoilers (recall the details of the *Westworld* Rickrolling Event) on social media sites or look things up on *Wikipedia*. Here the badness of spoiling is mitigated somewhat, as the person for whom the work is spoiled has chosen to have the work spoiled.

The second most common way of spoiling something for yourself is the way described above. You deduce some spoiler from some information that you have encountered. This information can be plot information, as in the example where you deduce that the butler did it, or it can be information about shooting locations, actor choices, statements made by the director, and so forth. When one spoils something for themselves in this manner, the question of whether the spoiling is bad is more complicated. It seems like there is nothing wrong in deducing that the butler did it, as described above. That's part of the fun of a good whodunit. That same goes for figuring out what will happen in a horror movie. Trying to deduce who will be the one to survive is almost as much fun as watching the action on screen. In other cases, however, deducing facts about films based on information that you come across can actually diminish your experience. Suppose that I didn't want to know (prior to seeing the movie) that Thanos is ultimately successful at the end of *Avengers: Infinity War*, but that I inadvertently deduced it from a number of tweets from actors in the film, none of which were spoilers on their own. Under these circumstances, I might actually be angry with myself for performing the deduction, given that I might have left the information well enough alone. This I would consider an instance of badness that I inflicted on myself.

As I mentioned, the third and fourth ways are not serious, but since we're considering ways in which spoiling is merely possible (as opposed to being either likely or probable), some far-fetched thought experiments are called for. The third way involves scenarios in which one spoils things for oneself, under circumstances in which one can anticipate future memory loss—here you intentionally spoil something for your future self. For example, suppose that someone is going to have to have their memory wiped (think *Eternal Sunshine of the Spotless Mind*, or some such), and just before the procedure leaves a bunch of notes that reveal the endings to all the great works listed in Appendix 1 (or for that matter, leaves a bunch of copies of Appendix 1 lying around) just for the purpose of spoiling things for their future self. While the technology is not currently available to do this, it's likely not terribly far off. Moreover, the example doesn't require this type of technology. Suppose that you're beginning to suffer degenerative memory loss. There are very few upsides to this type of thing occurring, but one of them is that you could re-experience the pleasure of reading their favorite books or watching their favorite shows again "for the first time." If you were to spoil these works, by leaving a bunch of notes with spoilers on them, it would certainly count as an instance of a morally bad spoiling.

The fourth way of spoiling something for yourself may turn out to be metaphysically impossible, and is certainly not possible at this time (although it is certainly logically possible). For those reasons I'll not go into a lot of detail on this one. Suffice it to say that if you invent a time machine, and are planning on eventually returning to the present time from the future, do yourself a solid and avoid details about future works of entertainment.

Are Some Works Too Bad to Spoil?

Our final tricky case involves works that are really bad. Recall that our primary criterion for determining whether a particular work makes the list of things that must never be spoiled is greatness. We naturally wonder whether this runs in the opposite direction. Is there a list of things that can always be spoiled in virtue of their being horrible? Are some works so bad that there is nothing about them that counts as spoilable?

There are some really horrible movies, television programs, and books out there. A quick Internet search will reveal dozens of lists of "worst books ever" or "worst movies of all time" or "worst television shows ranked," and so forth. These lists are pretty varied in their content, but there are certain works that almost always appear. On the worst movies list one almost always finds *Gigli*, *Showgirls*, and *From Justin to Kelly*. There are a handful of others that appear regularly, as well. If we take these to be representative really bad movies, can we conclude that it's okay to spoil these (or would have been when they were on their initial run)?

These are certainly not great films (huge understatement), but if we look at our definition of a spoiler we see that a spoiler (among other things) involves significant information, where significant was defined by reference to our "typical viewer" standard. So, to hold that these works can be spoiled at any time (or more precisely, that there is nothing legitimately spoilable about them), it would have to be the case that there is nothing that a typical viewer would find significant about them. I've not seen *Gigli*, but I have seen the others. In each case, there are at least some things that a typical viewer should find significant (not in a "bears on world affairs" sort of way, but in a "there are at least some interesting plot developments occurring" sort of way).

While the above movies do not fall into the category of things that it is always permissible to spoil, there are at least two films that come to mind that have absolutely no redeeming qualities—qualities that a typical viewer would consider to be significant: Eric Brevig's *Yogi Bear* and Dennis Dugan's *Grown Ups 2*. Feel free to spoil these at will.

You might object that even though there is nothing spoilable about these movies, some of the badness normally associated with spoiling might occur in particular cases. For example, if you tell a child that is waiting in line at the theater to see *Yogi Bear* that Jellystone Park gets shut down and Ranger Smith has to move out, then you've deprived that child of a particular experience that may be of value to them. The right thing to say here is that you shouldn't reveal that information as it violates the prohibition on revealing personal spoilers, but it doesn't actually reveal a legitimate spoiler.

A second worry for this view might involve movies that are considered to be truly horrific, and yet people love them. In fact, they love them in virtue of how bad they are. It's the old "so bad, it is good" category. The two paradigms of this category are Ed Wood's *Plan 9 from Outer Space* and Tommy Wiseau's *The Room*. These movies (and others on the list) are clearly important to a lot of people, and are included on both "truly horrible" lists and also "very favorite" lists. Given that, there is a clear prohibition on spoiling these works, but, paradoxically, if there were anything significant going on, then they wouldn't be held in such high regard, which means that it should be okay to spoil them. The resolution of the paradox lies in the fact that there is something significant in their badness (again, the total value of a work isn't just the sum of its aggregate parts). It is the rare "special" badness that is significant. This in turn makes these films spoilable.

In the case of *Yogi Bear*, we have a movie with no redeeming qualities, but nothing stands out about it as being laughably bad (the editing, lighting, writing, and other production values are all competent)—the film is just bad. In the case of our "so bad, it is good" films almost everything about the film-making stands out (the sets are ridiculous, the camera work is amateurish, sometimes the boom microphone is in the picture, and so on). This ultimately entails that works that are so bad that they can always be spoiled are not typically among the worst works. The very worst works (sometimes) end up being good.

14
Are Our Reactions to Spoilers Justified?

I've had many discussions with my students in recent years about how people react to spoilers. Most of the time their reaction to having something spoiled for them falls into one of three categories: 1. they get very upset, 2. they don't care at all, or 3. they're actually happy to have received the spoiler.

In my experience, people in the second category tend to not have much of an investment in the sorts of things that can be spoiled. They are not "into" popular culture. Sometimes people are in this category for "hoity toity" reasons—for example, because pop culture is beneath them—but usually, they are just uninterested in almost everything (except for maybe gossip or partying or whatever else otherwise uninterested college kids are into these days).

People in the third category are not uninterested; they just don't mind hearing spoilers. Usually, this is because of the sorts of reasons cited in the Leavitt-Christenfeld study: having the extra information in advance of their experiencing a particular work enhances their enjoyment of the work (or at a minimum doesn't diminish it). I'm not particularly concerned about people who fall into either category 2 or category 3. To each her own, as they say. I am, on the other hand, curious about people who fall into category 1.

You Know, There Are Worse Things than Spoiling

When I have these discussions with my students I'll ask them to raise their hands if they have ever been extremely upset because someone revealed a spoiler to them. In my large Introduction to Philosophy classes of about seventy students, typically twenty-five to thirty-five students will raise their hand. I'll then select an event that is currently going on in the world, that virtually everyone is aware of and everyone will agree is horrific, such as the plight of Syrian refugees or current famine conditions in sub-Saharan Africa, and ask them to keep their hands up, if they have ever been as upset (or even more upset) by that event as they were when something was spoiled for them. Surprisingly (to me, but apparently not to them) very few hands remain up—usually no more than five or ten.

The takeaway from this is that it appears that quite a few people in our society (perhaps more than half, if our college students are any indication) are more upset at having something spoiled than they are about famine, human rights violations, people with no place to live, and various other global atrocities.[1] This certainly raises some

---

[1] It's worth noting that the global atrocities I have chosen are ones that don't directly affect the persons to whom I've been asking these questions. Undoubtedly, they would be more concerned with things bearing directly on them, than they would be if a show they were watching got spoiled for them. So, when I discuss people's reactions to global atrocities, we can take that as meaning global atrocities that don't bear directly on their lives. Similarly, in raising these issues with my students I don't use examples of things that don't bear directly on their lives, but are currently a political hot issue. For example, many of my students on both sides of the political aisle have strong emotional reactions to US immigration policies, but, at

red flags. What does this tell us about our reactions to spoilers? Is our typical reaction to spoilers warranted, or are we overreacting? Given the facts about our reactions to spoilers (or at least the reactions of those of us who get pretty upset when spoilers are revealed to us) and people's reactions to global atrocities (again, noting that not everyone reacts poorly or with indifference to these sorts of things) there are four plausible assessments of our reactions: 1. we are reacting appropriately to both spoilers and global atrocities, 2. we are overreacting to spoilers, but have the appropriate response to global atrocities, 3. we are reacting appropriately to spoilers, but are not reacting strongly enough to global atrocities, and 4. we are not reacting appropriately to either spoilers or global atrocities.[2] Most people that I have discussed this with have the intuition that assessment 4 is the correct one. That is, most people believe that we should not have stronger reactions to spoilers than we have to global atrocities, and that our reactions to spoilers are perhaps too strong, while our reactions to global atrocities are not strong enough. I'm not, however, convinced that most people's intuitions are right on this issue. We'll see.

What Accounts for Our Reactions to Spoilers?

As I mentioned above, the students I've discussed this with do not find these results particularly surprising. The explanations that they give for why we react the way that we do to spoilers is quite illuminating. They also strike

---

least some of their passion on this issue, can be attributed to political tribalism, and not so much as a concern for those affected by said policies.

[2] There are other possible assessments of the situation, that are, simply, not plausible. For example, you could maintain that we are overreacting to global atrocities and but are not reacting strongly enough to having something spoiled.

me as being correct. Of course, there's no single reason that explains the disparity between our emotional reactions to having works spoiled and global atrocities, but there is a small set of responses that come up time and time again. We'll consider the four most often cited.[3] It's worth noting that three of these (investment, that it happens to you, and specifically what happens to you) sync up nicely with our account of the badness of spoiling. The other (proximity) serves to account for our relatively weak emotional reactions to global atrocities.

Most often when we have a negative emotional response to a work being spoiled, it is because of the investment that we have in that work. Recall that one of the worries that we raised for the Leavitt-Christenfeld study was that the subjects of the experiment were asked about works that were spoiled for them, but that they had no initial investment in This was relevant because some of the badness of spoiling has to do with harms related to our investment in works. For example, when you're deprived of something that you're invested in, you're deprived of something that you more strongly desire. The badness is amplified by the degree to which you're invested in a particular work. Deprivation is just one of the ways in which spoiling can yield badness. Other ways in which spoiling can be bad, such as desire frustration and experiential badness, are also affected by the degree to which you are invested in a particular work. Regarding

---

[3] There is a fifth response that arises pretty frequently, but it doesn't really address the discrepancy between our reactions to spoilers and our reactions to global atrocities, namely, that people aren't really as upset as they are claiming to be. Respondents maintain that people will take any opportunity to act indignant. This is a pretty interesting response, as none of my students admits to doing that themselves. Moreover, it seems that they believe that they are quite upset about having a spoiler revealed, but they don't believe that others get as upset as they do.

global atrocities that don't bear directly on their lives, many people just don't have much of an investment. That doesn't mean that they wouldn't prefer it if the global atrocity didn't exist; rather, they are just not "feeling it" as my students put it.

A second explanation often offered for why our reactions to spoilers are stronger than our reactions to certain global atrocities is that the spoiler happens to you, whereas the global atrocity does not. This explanation seems right. We don't become upset when we hear about something being spoiled for others. In fact, when the spoiler happens to someone else, our emotional response is back to being in line with our intuitions about how strongly we should react. If, for instance, I mention a case to my students in which someone was denied justice, they become moderately upset. If I tell them about a case in which something was spoiled for someone, they tend to snicker (in a "laughing at the poor fool" sort of way). Since the kind of global atrocities I'm using as test cases are by definition cases that do not bear on the lives of the students, it's not that surprising that their reactions are not as strong as they are to things that are, in fact, happening to them.

A third explanation has to do with proximity. Numerous studies show that physical proximity bears greatly on people's emotional response to events.[4] This accounts for the fact that our emotional responses to global atrocities are not only weaker than our responses to having things spoiled, but are also weaker than our responses to more local events that are not as horrific. If I tell my students about a person in our city that was sent to jail for a long

---

[4] See, for example, "The Effects of Proximity and Empathy on Ethical Decision-Making: An Exploratory Investigation" by J. Mencl and D.R. May in *Journal of Business Ethics* (2009) 85: 201.

period of time for either a minor crime or a crime that person did not commit, they tend to exhibit more empathy than they do for the plight of Syrian refugees or those living in famine conditions in Ethiopia. Probably both physical proximity and social proximity are in play here.

The fourth explanation is a close relative of the second. Not only is the fact that that it is happening to you a factor in why we have such emotionally charged responses to spoilers, but what is happening to you can be a factor. If someone accidentally reveals a spoiler, your emotional response is not as likely to be as strong as it is in cases where the spoiler is revealed on purpose. The students consider intentional reveals to be a form of disrespect. In some cases, your concerns are literally not being respected. In more extreme cases the person revealing the spoiler is doing so to be mean.[5] Conversely, the thing that is happening in the case of a global atrocity is not explicitly targeted at the students I've queried, so global atrocities don't engender this "I'm being harmed" or "I'm being disrespected" type of response.

What Constitutes an Appropriate Reaction?

These explanations, along with a few others, allow us to account for why we react to spoilers in the way that we do, and for why many of us have a stronger emotional reaction to spoilers than we have to global atrocities.[6] Notice, however, that the above explanations are descriptive in nature (as are pretty much all explanations), but they are not normative. In other words, these explanations tell us why we

---

[5] Again, there are an awful lot of jerks out there.

[6] Just so that no one gets the wrong idea. I'm way more bothered about global atrocities than I am about spoilers, but spoilers piss me off as well.

react to spoilers (and global atrocities) in the way that we do, but they don't tell us how we ought to react.

Perhaps the question of how we ought to react to spoilers, at least as far as our emotional responses go, is moot. In Section V of his *An Enquiry Concerning Human Understanding*, David Hume considers the question of how thoughts are different from beliefs.[7] Hume points out that we can think something without believing that thing to be true. For example, I can think the thought "Michael Myers died at the end of the new sequel to *Halloween*" without believing that Michael Myers died at the end of the new sequel to *Halloween*. In fact, it is not true, as is evidenced by the characteristic deep breathing that can be heard at the end of the credits. The difference, according to Hume, between merely thinking something (in the sense of just having the words run across your mind) and actually believing it, is that beliefs are essentially feelings. When we believe something, we feel it in a way. Hume makes this point in support of the position that beliefs are not something that we have any control over. For our purposes this is not relevant, but it is relevant that he thinks that feelings are not something that we have control over. On this point, I think Hume is correct. Try feeling differently about something. For example, if you are sad, you cannot just choose to not be sad. If you have unrequited feelings for someone, you cannot just stop having the feelings. Feelings are not the type of things we can turn on or off. So perhaps the question of how we should feel upon having a spoiler revealed is not something that is up to us. In which case, it doesn't make any sense to ask the question how *should* we react to spoilers (or global atroc-

---

[7] S. Buckle, ed., *Hume: An Enquiry Concerning Human Understanding: And Other Writings* (Cambridge Texts in the History of Philosophy) (Cambridge: Cambridge University Press, 2007).

ities). The way you feel is just the way you feel.

While I'm completely sympathetic to Hume's point here, I don't think the fact that feelings cannot be turned on or off and that our immediate emotional responses to things that happen is somewhat beyond our control, is sufficient to render the normative question of how we ought to respond to things moot. Hume's position regarding belief formation is known as "doxastic involuntarism." Doxastic involuntarism is the view that we don't choose our beliefs. Even the most die-hard doxastic involuntarists would acknowledge that we can do things to influence the beliefs that we form. For example, suppose that I don't currently have any beliefs about voodoo zombies. I can't just choose to believe things about voodoo zombies. That said, if I choose to read a book about voodoo zombies, I will certainly begin to form beliefs about them. So even though belief formation on this view is involuntary, we can do things to influence the formation of beliefs. Similarly, even though our emotional responses to things such as spoilers might be out of our immediate control, we can do things to influence how we respond subsequently. For example, you might choose to spend a great deal of time thinking about your priorities regarding spoilers, or thinking about how much time you have invested in certain programs, books, or movies. A change in priorities or in level of emotional investment, might lead to different responses in the future. The payoff of all this is that even though our emotional responses to certain things might be automatic, that doesn't mean that there are not normative issues at play in how we respond to things. So, we can set aside the worry that the question of how we ought to respond to spoilers is moot.

-----
[8] Aristotle. *Aristotle: Nicomachean Ethics* (Cambridge Texts in the History of Philosophy) (Cambridge: Cambridge University Press, 2000).

So, what is the appropriate emotional response to spoilers? While few philosophers have written extensively on the topic of spoilers (perhaps just one), there has been much written on the emotions and emotional responses to things. For our purposes, Aristotle's account seems to be spot on. In his work, *Nicomachean Ethics,* Aristotle discusses what it is to be virtuous.[8] According to Aristotle's view, virtues are excellences of human beings in which rational activity is made possible. They are what allow us to be rational creatures, which, for Aristotle, is basically our main purpose. Part of the trick to becoming virtuous is having precisely the right emotions under particular circumstances. Aristotle expresses this in what has come to be known as "The Doctrine of the Mean." The idea is that sometimes you need emotions in order for reason to operate, and either too much emotion, too little emotion, or having the wrong kind of emotion can prevent reason from expressing itself.

So how does this apply to spoilers? I propose that Aristotle would be of the opinion that someone who is completely stoical upon having a spoiler revealed to them does not have enough emotion. Perhaps they wouldn't be inclined to make it known that they didn't appreciate hearing the spoiler or that they wouldn't appreciate having it happen again (or their words may convey those things, but their lack of emotion renders their words without any persuasive force). At the other extreme, we have too much emotion. We've already seen how that can turn out: we might end up putting a knife in someone's chest. Aristotle would admonish us to have the right amount of emotion as is warranted by the situation. For Aristotle, the Doctrine of the Mean doesn't require that we have an emotional response that is exactly halfway between two extremes. Rather, he calls for a mean relative to our particular circumstances.

Circumstances, of course, can vary from person to person. So, the amount that you should be upset by having something spoiled should be proportional to your investment in the work that is spoiled, and the amount of badness you incur upon having something spoiled. So, in my case, learning that FBI agent Teddy Daniels in *Shutter Island* is really mental asylum inmate Andrew Laeddis should appropriately yield a much tamer emotional response than my learning that in *Carnival of Souls* Mary Henry had been dead the whole time, since I enjoy horror films considerably more than I enjoy psychological thrillers. I would be harmed more to learn the horror story spoiler than I would be to learn the psychological thriller spoiler. Conversely, some with different preferences should have a different emotional response.

The payoff of this is: if Aristotle, as I have interpreted him here, is right, then it seems that the emotional reaction my students have to spoilers is not unwarranted. It's the right sort of response, given their interest in not having things spoiled for them. It's also appropriate that different students have different responses to spoilers, and that some students even fall into categories 2 and 3 as explicated above.

I like to think of it this way: art is important to many of us, so our strong emotional reactions to art are justified. This includes both our reactions to the works of art themselves—the way the art makes us feel, when we encounter it—as well as our reactions to having the works of art spoiled for us. Regarding the disparity between the way many of us react to spoilers and global atrocities, the right thing to say is that we shouldn't temper our reactions to having things spoiled; rather, we should be reacting more strongly to things happening in the world that don't bear directly on our lives.

15
Culture, Relativism, and Spoilers

As we've established, there exists a pretty strong *prima facie* prohibition against revealing spoilers. Our examination of the history of spoilers in Chapter 1 makes it clear that recognition of that prohibition is a relatively recent phenomenon. Fifty or so years ago people were just beginning to realize that there is a badness to spoiling. Evidence for this lies in the fact that at the end of movies such as *Psycho* and *Les Diaboliques* the directors felt they had to admonish people not to reveal the surprise endings. Moreover, as was mentioned in Chapter 2 not all cultures recognize the prohibition against revealing spoilers. For example, while traveling in Ghana in 2018 I had the occasion to discuss spoilers with several of the local citizens. Without exception, they did not feel the force of our concern about spoilers—it just didn't seem like a big deal to them—and they did not consider that there was anything wrong with revealing spoilers. The situation there is not unlike the situation in the United States during my childhood, except that the Ghanaians weren't in a rush to spoil things for one another (probably because 1. they weren't interested in being jerks, and 2. the people I spoke with in Ghana were all adults). This raises the question of whether the *prima facie* prohibition against revealing spoilers applies universally—at all locations and times— or whether it's a cultural thing, that can vary from time to time as a particular culture changes (as did ours), and can vary from culture to culture when two cultures' attitudes about spoiling differ from one another.

Spoiling Ethics or Spoiling Etiquette?

Since the prohibition against spoiling involves a normative claim, namely, that one ought not to reveal legitimate spoilers, it will be useful to identify the type of normative claim that is being made. That is, what sort of normative institution issues admonitions pertaining to spoilers? One normative institution that makes demands on the ways in which we behave is the law. The law admonishes us not to behave in a variety of ways. Currently, however, there are no laws on the books that refer to spoilers, so we can quickly dismiss the law as being the source of the prohibition against revealing spoilers.

A more serious candidate is etiquette. Etiquette is a normative institution that tells how we should or should not behave in a variety of situations. The question that we want to consider is whether or not revealing spoilers is merely a matter of meeting the demands of etiquette.[1] There are certainly reasons for thinking that not revealing spoilers is a matter of etiquette. People consider the revealing of spoilers to be in bad taste. People have strong reactions to spoilers, but they don't want to legislate against revealing spoilers, which is something that often

---

[1] I say "merely" here because it is possible that certain normative claims may get their authority from more than one normative institution. Committing murder, for example, is not only illegal and unethical, it's also rude. So, we see that the law, ethics, and etiquette tell us not to commit murder.

happens when people consider something to be unethical. The fact that attitudes about spoiling vary from culture to culture is a hallmark of etiquette. Note, however, that each of these is consistent with the revealing of spoilers also issuing from ethics, which is a normative institution, as well. People tend to frown at unethical behavior, certain unethical behaviors, such as lying, are behaviors that we are not inclined to make illegal, and attitudes toward ethical issues vary from culture to culture (for example, attitudes about the permissibility of abortion, the death penalty, and euthanasia vary greatly around the world).[2]

So, the issue to be sorted out is whether revealing spoilers is solely a matter of etiquette, or whether it is either solely a matter of ethics, or matter of both etiquette and ethics. If it is solely a matter of etiquette, then we have an answer to the question of whether there exists a universal prohibition against the revealing of spoilers. Since the rules of etiquette vary from culture to culture, then necessarily a universal prohibition does not exist.[3] Even if all cultures were to have an identical rule regarding spoilers, there would not exist a universal prohibition against revealing spoilers; rather, it would just be a coincidence that the prohibition was held unanimously and uniformly (which would be subject to change as long as cultural values change). If, on the other hand, the prohibition on spoiling issues from ethics (either

---

[2] Of course, there are laws against perjury and against fraud, but those are highly specific, and do not constitute a general law against lying.

[3] This is not to suggest that all differences in etiquette occur at the level of culture; rather, it's just a convenient way of talking about differences. Moreover, since our concern is a difference in attitudes regarding spoilers that exists at a cultural level, it is also useful for our purposes to carve them up in this way. In reality things are much more complicated than that. The norms of etiquette can also issue from particular subcultures, regions, cliques, industries, organizations, professions, and so on.

solely or in combination with etiquette), then the matter will require further unpacking.

Examining the purpose of each institution holds the key to determining which institution or institutions issues the prohibition against spoiling. Etiquette primarily exists as a normative institution in order to facilitate social interactions. It's a way of making things run smoothly, which allows us to not worry about how certain behaviors are going to be received. The rules of etiquette are mostly arbitrary. Consider the prohibition that exists in some cultures against putting your elbows on the table at which you are dining. A posture that casual might signal to others that you are relaxed and enjoying yourself, which is ultimately a compliment to others. On the other hand, it might signal to others that you lack respect for the others at the table, by taking an inordinate amount of space or not affording the situation the formality it deserves, which are not compliments. Having a rule of etiquette solves the dilemma you might find yourself in: not knowing how the action (or the failure to act in that way) will be received by others. Some cultures deem it to be a violation of etiquette and others do not. There is not a right answer as to whether you objectively ought to refrain from putting your elbows on the table. As long as you know the rules of the culture that you are in, then you are okay, and it doesn't matter one way or the other how a particular society comes down on the issue.

By contrast, ethics is a normative institution that exists to regulate behaviors as they bear on the welfare of other beings. The moral prohibition on murder, for example, doesn't exist so that people will know whether or not murder is expected of them in a given situation, as it would if murder were simply a matter of etiquette; rather, it exists because in most instances murder bears negatively on the welfare of others. The same is also true for the prohibitions against lying, cheating, stealing, and so forth.

The difference in the respective purposes of etiquette and ethics provides us with a very good reason for thinking that regardless of whether there are etiquette-based prohibitions against revealing spoilers, there are certainly ethics-based prohibitions against spoiling. This was established in Section II, when we were able to identify the various ways in which spoiling can be bad, and the harms that spoiling yields.

Is the Ethical Prohibition against Spoiling Relative?

While we've established that revealing spoilers is not just a matter of etiquette, we've not established that the prohibition against revealing spoilers applies universally. That depends on whether ethics is objective and universal or is relative in some sense. If ethics is objective, then the prohibitions that exist in our culture would be applicable in other cultures, as well (or, conversely, the lack of prohibition against revealing spoilers that exists elsewhere, would be applicable here, either way with respect to spoiling, things should stand and fall together, as it were). On the other hand, if morality is relative, say, relative to cultures, then there is no reason to suppose that a moral prohibition that exists in one part of the world has any bearing on the morality of the same action in other parts of the world. The same would be true for a prohibition that exists in a particular culture at a particular point in time. Over time, as the culture changes, there is no expectation that the culture's values remain constant, so there is no expectation that the prohibition would continue to exist.

While the issue of whether there are universal moral truths is still widely debated among scholars (at least in certain circles), my position is that the debate is pretty much settled. The main arguments for ethical relativism have been well exposed over the years, and the view looks pretty untenable.[4] For our purposes, the appropriate relativist position to look at is cultural ethical relativism, as we are wondering whether the moral rules for revealing spoilers varies from culture to culture. The main argument for cultural ethical relativism, as James Rachels points out, is the failed Cultural Differences Argument.[5] This is an argument that emerged from anthropologists who concluded from the fact that different cultures have different moral beliefs, that there must not be any objective moral truths. It was on the basis of this argument, in particular, that cultural ethical relativism began to gain acceptance. It has been rightly pointed out, however, that just because people have different beliefs about something, it doesn't follow that there are no objective facts about that thing. For example, different cultures have held different beliefs about the number of Gods that exist, but it doesn't follow that there is no objective fact about the number of Gods that exist.[6]

Moreover, we have good reason for thinking that there should be a universal prohibition against spoiling, namely, that spoiling demonstrably yields bad consequences, and, hence, is demonstrably bad. We've already seen a number of ways in which revealing a spoiler can lead to harms. So even if the person for whom the work is spoiled lives at a

---

[4] For a thorough discussion of why various forms of relativism (including moral relativisms) fail, see Thomas Nagel's *The Last Word* (New York: Oxford University Press), 1997.

[5] James Rachels "The Challenge of Cultural Relativism" in *The Elements of Moral Philosophy*, fifth edition (New York: McGraw-Hill), 2006.

[6] I actually know whether God exists, but I'm not going to tell you, as that would be a spoiler. You are just going to have to wait until you die to find out (or not find out, depending).

time or in a place where people are not apt to be as upset upon hearing a spoiler as folks currently are in the United States, they still have the potential for a diminished experience upon engaging the spoiled work, and are still deprived of the experience of engaging the work in an unspoiled fashion. So, the right thing to conclude is that as long as a practice leads to demonstrable badness, and there is no good consequence to weigh against it, there must exist a *prima facie* moral prohibition against that practice.

To deny this last point is essentially to maintain that as long as a group of people feels that something is acceptable or something is unacceptable, then that thing is acceptable or it is unacceptable, and that consequences are not relevant. Suppose that a majority of people in a culture were on board with really horrific acts such as mass shootings. You could imagine people in a particular culture saying things like, "Well, mass shootings don't happen too often, and everybody needs to blow off a little steam from time to time. It's good that we have them!" Presumably, we would want to correct their view, get them to stop allowing them to occur, and, most importantly, recognize that they are morally wrong, precisely because of the badness that they yield. Admittedly, this example is a bit far-fetched (since I'm not aware of any examples of cultures that actually like mass shootings), but there are plenty of cases in which large groups of people believe that certain actions are morally okay, when they clearly are not. At one time in the United States, for example, a majority of people felt that slavery was morally okay. There are still societies in which a majority of people maintain that it is permissible for men to beat their wives (under various circumstances). It is not far-fetched to suppose that large groups of people can be wrong about moral issues. The view that bad consequences are not relevant to the moral permissibility of an action is, simply, implausible.

First World Problems

In response to this someone might object that if pretty much everyone in a given culture is okay with spoiling, then, even if there is a prohibition against it, it should be viewed as acceptable. It is as if everyone has waived their right to object, or some such. This is where things get a bit tricky. On the one hand, we've just been given an argument to the effect that spoiling should be viewed as universally bad, because it can lead to bad consequences, even in parts of the world where people don't have the intuition that it is a bad thing to do. Again, a bunch of people believing that something is okay doesn't make it okay. On the other hand, there is something that doesn't quite ring true with maintaining that groups cannot decide for themselves whether things like spoiling are socially acceptable—if no one truly cares, why should we (especially since we are not talking about badness on the order of murder)? To the extent that we want our theoretical account of the badness of spoiling to be in reflective equilibrium with our common-sense intuitions about spoiling, including when it is okay to spoil, it would be good if there were some way to reconcile these facts.

It would be *ad hoc* to simply reject one of these in favor of the other. Fortunately, to the extent that our theoretical account is somewhat nuanced, there is a way of giving due weight and reverence to both the position that spoiling is universally morally bad and the intuition that spoiling should be considered acceptable in certain cultures, without having to abandon either. Our reconciliation begins with the observation that the badness of things doesn't just occur in a vacuum. For any bad phenomenon, it does not simply have an amount that it is bad. It's more complicated than that. Things are bad for individuals, and the degree to which they are bad varies for each individual.

For example, on occasion I like to prepare a nice meal for my friends and family. I always do this with the hope that they will enjoy the meal, and perhaps even make a little bit of a fuss about it. They usually do, but if they don't I don't consider it to be terribly bad, as I don't really experience much badness under the circumstances. I have a friend, however, who is a professional chef. When he prepares a meal for friends he has considerably more invested in the outcome, than I do when I prepare a meal. If he doesn't get the response he was looking for he actually gets offended and his feelings are hurt. Under the circumstances, he experiences considerably more badness than I experience under similar circumstances. So, the degree to which something can be bad can vary quite a bit from person to person.

The amount of badness people experience can also vary for a particular person depending on what other things are occurring in that person's life at the time. So, for example, when my favorite football team is not doing well, I usually experience some badness (not moral badness, but badness just the same).[7] If things are mostly going well in my life, this badness is exacerbated quite a bit. I become considerably more invested in things like sports, when I don't have other things to worry about. Conversely, when I have a bunch of other bad things going on, then I'm less affected by the outcome of sporting events. This can happen when there are many other bad things going on, or just a few bad things going on, but ones that are considerably worse. The payoff of this is that the badness an individual experiences from almost any particular thing can be dwarfed by some other badness, in one circumstance,

---

[7] As I mentioned, it's the San Francisco 49ers, so I've become quite used to the badness in recent years. But back in the 1980s . . .

but not dwarfed in other circumstances. Not having enough funds in your checking account to pay all your bills might seem like a really bad thing in normal situations, but not seem bad at all when you are grieving the death of a loved one, or your country is occupied, or you are facing jail time. In summary, there are a number of factors that might serve to mitigate the amount of badness that some particular action yields for some individual.

If we apply this to spoiling in places such as Ghana, where most citizens have more immediate concerns (there is widespread poverty and many citizens have little or no access to the most minimal forms of health care) than whether or not a particular work is spoiled for them, we can say that spoiling is bad for Ghanaians in the objective sense, but that the badness gets dwarfed by a number of more significant issues. Spoiling is a first-world problem in every sense of the expression. This not only resolves the tension between our theoretical account of the badness of spoiling and our common-sense intuitions regarding different cultures rightly having different values regarding spoiling, but it works well with the account that we gave in Chapter 14: the lack of badness experienced by some when something is spoiled for them reflects the lack of investment they have in that thing.

In situations where a lack of investment doesn't exist, we don't want to hold that revealing spoilers is not bad (assuming that the badness isn't dwarfed by something else), even if no one thinks it bad. I have in mind the circumstance described in the opening pages of this book, where my friends would race to spoil things for one another. No one at the time considered spoiling to be bad (again, we didn't exactly have the concept), but we all experienced badness when it happened. Since we were invested in certain works in the 1960's spoiling was bad then. So, when my friend said "Did you see *Voyage to the Bottom of the Sea* this week? The Seaview was attacked by a werewolf!" he diminished my future viewing experience, and that experience was not dwarfed by something. It plain sucked!

16
What to Do When You Encounter Someone Who Spoils

At this point it should be pretty clear that one hundred percent of the badness of spoiling can be attributed to the spoiler revealer. The person who is on the receiving end of an unsolicited spoiler is a victim, of sorts. While we certainly don't want to engage in anything like victim blaming or suggest that victims are even partially responsible for the ways in which they've been victimized, there are things we can do to minimize the amount of spoiling that we experience: we can do things to avoid spoilers, and we can do things to deter would-be spoilers. Taking the proper precautions and dealing with those who spoil can, in the long run, help put an end to what is clearly a callous, ugly, and ultimately disrespectful stain on our society.

How to Avoid Spoilers

A phenomenon that occurs with some regularity these days is folks announcing that they are avoiding social media for some period of time so as to avoid having things spoiled for them. This typically happens when a new book, television show, or movie is coming out, and there is enough buzz surrounding the work that people can reasonably anticipate that there will likely be numerous spoilers posted on Facebook, Twitter, and Instagram, etc. This occurs, for example, when a new installment in the *Marvel Cinematic Universe* or *Star Wars* franchises are released. It also occurs when new seasons of *The Walking Dead* and *Game of Thrones* premiere. It was also fairly common (but lesser so, due to its being a while ago) when the *Harry Potter* books and movies came out. Sometimes the amount of time that one must stay off social media in order to avoid spoilers can be pretty extensive. By contrast, one doesn't see this phenomenon occurring when things being released are not considered to be "events" (a new installment in the *Saw* franchise is not likely to elicit a bunch of spoilers on social media, nor is a new Tom Hanks movie or a new James Patterson novel). While one generally has control over when they can engage a new work (how long after it is released they get to see or read it), it's not just once the work has been released that one is at risk of having it spoiled. In the case of the works listed above that are likely to elicit spoilers on social media, spoilers often begin being revealed with relative frequency several weeks ahead of the work being available to the general public (again, I'm looking at you, Mr. Mark Hamill).[1] Staying off social media can be an effective, albeit, not foolproof, way of avoiding spoilers, but it comes at a pretty high cost. One misses out on the value of social media, which, for some, can be pretty substantial. Moreover, some folks are not in a position to stay off social media. As someone who directs a university ethics institute (The Richard Richards Institute for Ethics), is the Executive Board Chair of the Intercollegiate Ethics Bowl,

---

[1] Mark Hamill's attempts at being cryptic on social media have led to more spoiler reveals than we care to think about.

and produces and co-hosts two podcasts, part of my job is to have a daily presence on social media.[2]

Since simply avoiding social media is a good, but not optimal, strategy for avoiding spoilers, let's look as some other strategies that can either supplement or replace avoiding social media as part of a successful strategy.

How to Deal with Spoiler Revealers

A great strategy for avoiding spoilers is to simply be that person who sees everything and reads everything first. This is a lesson that I learned pretty early on. When my friends and I would race to be the one who spoiled things for others, the trick was always a matter of getting there first (that's pretty much how races work). There are, however, numerous drawbacks with this strategy. To begin with, given the sheer volume of pop culture there is to be consumed, it's not possible to engage everything first. You can, of course, do this with the handful of things that you're most interested in, but it's not possible to do this with everything. There just aren't enough hours in the day. If you have any semblance of a life, it becomes nearly impossible to engage those works you're most interested in in a timely fashion. Moreover, this strategy doesn't help with those aforementioned reveals that are out there in advance of the official release date of certain works. Still, there is a good message there: you can avoid quite a few spoilers by engaging works that you don't want to have spoiled as early as possible.

---

[2] The podcasts are *I Think, Therefore I Fan Podcast*, and *Ethics Bowl, The Podcast*. I'm now wondering whether this footnote isn't just one great big shameless plug. It's an interesting question, that it's probably best to not consider.

Another strategy is to identify those people in your social media circles, such as Cassandra, who routinely reveal spoilers and unfollow them. This gives you control over when you see other people's posts. On Facebook, unfollowing doesn't even require unfriending—they never even know that you've done it. A related strategy involves avoiding both fan pages and fans. If you follow fan pages on Facebook, you'll receive everything posted on those pages. With certain fan pages, you can choose to look at them when you want to without actually following the page. Some pages are "closed group" pages, however, which means that you can only see the content if you are a member. Under those circumstances, you must choose whether it's worth it being a member of the group, when that entails that you will occasionally be exposed to spoilers. Most often with groups of this type, you can simply turn off notifications during those periods just before and just after a work that is likely to elicit spoilers is released. Avoiding fans is a little more demanding, since it's not the kind of thing that you can do in a stealthy or covert fashion. If the fan is someone close, they will, in all likelihood, know that they are being avoided. My advice here is to do this sort of thing sparingly (at least in the case of fans who are close friends or family members). Sure, spoilers are a huge issue, but friendships and good family relationships are at least slightly more important.

Another strategy for avoiding spoilers is to talk to the people in your life who might spoil something and tell them the specific things you don't want spoiled, as well as the general things that you don't want spoiled. While there are plenty of jerks out there, they are well in the minority. Most people will be happy to oblige. Moreover, most people who reveal spoilers are not aware that they're doing it, or they're not aware that it is bad to do so, or they're not aware that they are the sort of person who continually spoils, and so forth. By talking to them you will likely be doing them a solid. The final strategy for avoiding spoilers is to know the profile of a spoiler revealer.

But Spoiler Revealers Look Just Like Everybody Else

Spoiler revealers don't fit an exact profile. Still, there are types that are more inclined to reveal spoilers. If you're aware of the type of person who's likely to be a spoiler revealer, then you can take precautions to avoid spoilers when it is critical to do so.

Children, for example, are notorious spoilers (perhaps the most egregious spoiler revealers of all). They don't generally possess the concept that spoiling is bad (they don't even think of spoilers as spoilers), but they are dying to tell you every little detail of movies, shows, and books that they like. If you are waiting to see one of those programs or movies that have intergenerational appeal (such as a film based on a comic book), then you want to avoid children at all costs.

People who do not identify as fans are, all things being equal, more likely to reveal spoilers. They tend to not feel the gravity or significance of the various works, to the extent that fanboys and fangirls do, so they are generally not as aware of the badness of spoiling. It is a function of not being sufficiently cognizant of the investment that some people have in various works. The further away one gets from fan status, the more likely that one is to reveal spoilers.

Not to suggest that fanboys and fangirls can't also be spoiler revealers. There's a certain type of fan whose identity is so tied to being a fan (either of a particular show or movie series or just being a fan of pop culture in general) that they wear their fandom like a badge of honor. In my experience, this particular type of fanboy or fangirl is more apt to reveal spoilers than the average person, as it is another tool in their "Hey, look at me! I'm a huge fan!" arsenal.

Many people are spoiler revealers out of a sort of cluelessness about the badness of spoiling, but some folks spoil maliciously. If you know that someone is a jerk in general, and especially if they are the sort of jerk who derives pleasure from ruining things for others, then this is a person who has a greater than average potential for being a spoiler revealer. It is nearly impossible to avoid jerks completely (some of them work where we work, some live in our neighborhoods, some of them are at our schools), but to the extent you can, when major works are released you will find it worth while to put forth the effort.

There are other general "types" who are more apt to be spoiler revealers. There are people who simply have no filter. With this type of person, if something pops in their head, it comes out of their mouth. If you have a friend like this and you know that she has recently read a book that you are about to read or has seen a show that you are about to see, then at least know the risk you are putting yourself in by interacting with this person. Closely related to the "no filter" type are people who either just can't help but to post on social media everything they think or feel and people who are too invested in certain works (think Cassandra here), such that they cannot help but post spoilers on social media. Finally, there is the type of person who assumes that others know everything that they know (or have seen everything that they have seen or have read everything that they have read, and so forth). What each of these types has in common, in addition to being more likely to be a spoiler revealer, is that none of them spoils maliciously. They just can't help it.

How to Deal with Spoiler Revealers

We've certainly come a long way in the last fifty or sixty years or so with respect to spoilers. As a society we have developed a strong sense of what constitutes a legitimate spoiler, how bad it is to spoil things for others, and what sorts of things should never be spoiled. Spoilers are definitely part of our collective consciousness. And yet, spoilers and spoiler revealers are still a problem. This raises the question of how to deal with those who continue to reveal spoilers.

Since most spoiler reveals don't issue from bad intentions, it's not just a matter of punishing those who spoil. So, what to do when you encounter someone who spoils? What's the appropriate way to respond to spoilers?

One option is to just let it slide. This is not, however, an acceptable option. If the spoiler revealer isn't made aware of the badness of their actions, then they will spoil again. We have an obligation to others to do what we can anytime we interact with a spoiler revealer.

Another option is to say something like "Hey, spoiler alert!" Since it is likely that the spoiler revealer already is aware of spoilers and that spoiling is a bad thing to do, it is unlikely that this approach will do much to deter future spoilings.

What is required, then is something more forceful. Something like a brief discussion of just how bad it is to spoil things for others, along with some explanation of why it is bad. If that doesn't work, then purchase a copy of this book for them. Presumably, that will do the trick. If it doesn't, and the person continues to reveal spoilers, an intervention or even a spoiler exorcism may be warranted. Whatever you do, even if they tell you that Snape killed Dumbledore, that Norman Bates is Mother, and that the Planet of the Apes is Earth, you must not stab them in the chest!

The Lists

Appendix 1
The Thirty Greatest
Spoilers of All Time

1. In **Psycho** the audience has seen the murderous Mother on several occasions (but always from angles that don't reveal her face) and has heard her speak on several others, so it is extremely shocking when Lila Crane spins Mother to face her, revealing that she is a long-since-dead rotting corpse. A second shocking moment immediately follows when the audience realizes as Norman Bates bursts into the room dressed as Mother that he was Mother the entire time.

2. **Planet of the Apes** (1968 version) ends with Taylor and Nova leaving Zira, Cornelius, Dr. Zaius and the others to make a new life for themselves away from ape civilization in the Forbidden Zone. The movie is seemingly over until the camera pans out exposing the ruins of the Statue of Liberty, revealing that they had been on a post-atomic-war Earth the entire time.

3. In Agatha Christie's novel **Murder on the Orient Express** detective Hercule Poirot reveals that all the many suspects had taken part together in the killing of Ratchett

(a.k.a. Cassetti), who was responsible for the abduction and murder of Daisy Armstrong. A second great twist occurs when Poirot lets the killers decide for themselves which of two stories they will tell the police (the true one or one that doesn't implicate them).

4. During the much-anticipated light-saber battle between Darth Vader and Luke Skywalker in *The Empire Strikes Back*, Darth reveals to Luke that he is his father. Luke doesn't take the news all that well.

5. In *Harry Potter and the Half-Blood Prince*, Harry and Dumbledore are ambushed by Draco Malfoy, who intends on killing Dumbledore. Malfoy gets Dumbledore's wand. It seems pretty hopeless for Dumbledore, but Malfoy ultimately doesn't have it in him to finish the job. It appears that Dumbledore will survive, until suddenly and unexpectedly (at least far as the reader's expectations are concerned) Snape enters the room and kills Dumbledore, himself.

6. In Agatha Christie's second top ten appearance on this list, *The Murder of Roger Ackroyd*, revealing the murderer involves a double twist. The murderer is the story's narrator who is none other than Hercule Poirot's assistant, Dr. Sheppard.

7. In what is arguably one of the five best episodes of *The Twilight Zone* an alien race, the Kanamits, is taking humans back to their home planet. The humans have been lulled into a false sense of security in part by the Kanamits' book *To Serve Man*. In the penultimate scene, cryptographer Michael Chambers reveals that *To Serve Man* is a cookbook, and that the humans are not headed to a paradise, after all.

8. *Carnival of Souls* is one of the first, in what has now become many movies, in which the main character has been, unbeknownst to the viewing audience, dead the entire time. In this case, it is revealed at the end of the film that Mary Henry died in the car crash that she appeared to survive at the beginning of the film.

9. *Soylent Green* is believed to be made of a high protein plankton which can be used to feed people in a future dominated by extreme overpopulation. The big reveal, of course, is that Soylent Green is people.

10. *Fight Club* provides an interesting twist on the "the main character was dead the whole time" theme by giving us the "the main character never existed the whole time" theme. The ending of the movie reveals that Tyler Durden is just a fiction in the mind of The Narrator.

11. *Avengers: Infinity War* makes the list, not so much for something completely surprising, but for the sheer number of *Marvel Cinematic Universe* superheroes who are killed by Thanos. When Thanos snapped his finger killing Dr. Strange, Spiderman, Black Panther, Groot (who dies in about fifty percent of the films he is in) and Bucky Barnes to name a few, MCU fans were stunned.

12. At the end of the film *The Wizard of Oz* it is revealed that Dorothy's trip to Oz was all a dream, that she had sustained a head injury in the twister, and was just at that moment regaining consciousness.

13. In *Les Diaboliques* you believe for most of the film that Nicole Horner and Christina Delassalle have murdered Michel Delassalle. This changes when Michel's not being dead scares Christina to death, literally (she has a

heart attack). The surprise is that it was Nicole and Michel who were conspiring to kill Christina (who was known to have a heart condition) the whole time. A further twist comes at the very end when a boy reports that Christina has returned his slingshot to him, rendering it unclear whether Christina actually died.

14. In *Saw*, Jigsaw—the evil mastermind of the film series' torture scenarios—has set up a situation in which two men are chained to pipes in a skeevy bathroom. To escape they must saw through their own bones with rusty hacksaws. On the floor between them is a corpse. At the end of the movie the corpse rises and reveals himself to be Jigsaw.

15. The big spoiler revealer in *The Crying Game* is that unbeknownst to Fergus, Dil (with whom Fergus falls in love) is a transgender woman. Today this would not even count as mildly shocking (nor should it). It's something that occurs relatively frequently in film and literature, and it certainly would not be played as something shocking. In 1992, however, audiences were stunned. The film delivered the twist to great effect, as it completely transformed the film from a political thriller to a love story.

16. In the final scene in *Casablanca* it appears that Rick Blaine and Ilsa Lund are going to escape Casablanca and rekindle their romance. Surprisingly, Rick holds Louis Renault at gunpoint while Victor Laszlo and Ilsa escape. It was perhaps Rick's first truly selfless act in years.

17. Until the big reveal at the end, it appears that *Shutter Island* is a film about an FBI agent, Teddy Daniels, investigating a disappearance at an insane asylum. Eventually it is revealed that Daniels is, in fact, Andrew Laeddis, Shutter Island's most dangerous inmate.

18. The great thing about the surprise twist in *Se7en* is the way in which it is woven into the plot. Each of the killings in the film is related to one of the seven deadly sins. The reveal is that the head in the box is that of Tracy, the wife of the detective-protagonist David Mills. The killer, John Doe, killed Tracy (who in a second surprise was pregnant), because he was envious of Mills's relationship with his wife. This caused Mills to kill Doe, exhibiting the final deadly sin—wrath.

19. In *The Wicker Man* (1973 version) Neil Howie travels to Summerisle (a remote island) to search for a missing girl he comes to believes is intended to be a victim of ritual sacrifice. The twist is that he has been lured to the island so that the island's pagans can sacrifice him.

20. *The Village* appears to be a period piece in which residents of a nineteenth-century village live in fear of the monsters that reside in the woods just outside the village. In the end it is revealed that it is not the nineteenth century, and that the villagers have been deceived the whole time.

21. Perhaps the best known of the "the main character was dead the whole time" films is *The Sixth Sense*. Few, at the time saw it coming that Malcom Crowe had been murdered at the beginning of the movie, despite the fact that he was working with a boy who had the ability to see dead people.

22. In *The Usual Suspects* Verbal Kint spends the entire movie providing details about a crime to Agent Dave Kujan. The twist comes once Kint is released. He is revealed to be Keyser Söze, the mastermind of the crime. Moreover, nearly the entirety of Kint's story (and by extension, much of the film) was a fabrication, the elements of which came from insignificant details in Kujan's office.

23. In what is perhaps the greatest ending to a television series ever, Dick Loudin who is Bob Newhart's character on *Newhart* wakes up in bed with Emily Hartley, played by Suzanne Pleshette, on the set of *The Bob Newhart Show*. He is now Bob Hartley. He turns to her and says "Honey, Honey wake up You won't believe the dream I just had."

24. **The Others** is another "they were dead the whole time" story. In this one Grace Stewart and her two children are living in a house they believe to be haunted by spirits. The twist is that they are the spirits (they sort of manage to haunt themselves, but not in a way that is as silly as it sounds). In a further twist it is revealed that Grace killed the children and then committed suicide.

25. In **Primal Fear** the audience believes that Aaron Stampler, who has been accused of murder, is not responsible for the murders, as he suffers from dissociative identity disorder, and that it is his evil alter-identity, Roy, who commits the crimes. Once he is found innocent by reason of insanity, it is revealed that Stampler is faking the disorder, and that it is Roy who is real (not Aaron).

26. In the final scene of **Night of the Living Dead** it appears that the zombies have lost the battle and that the film's hero, Ben, has managed to survive. The surprise ending comes as Ben is mistaken for a zombie and shot in the head by one of the non-zombies who are combing the area in order to kill the remaining zombies.

27. Even though the big reveal is hinted at by the film's title, it still came as a surprise to most viewers of **American Psycho** that Patrick Bateman (perhaps) didn't actually murder those whom he thought he had murdered. At least one of the killings, and possibly all of them occurred solely in his head.

28. For a season and a half, fans of the television series *Twin Peaks* wondered who killed Laura Palmer. In a twist, the killer turned out to be her father, Leland Palmer. In another twist the killer was not exactly her father, but, rather, some evil spirit named "Bob" who had inhabited her father's body.

29. The clever twist in *Orphan* is that the evil orphan, Esther, is actually a thirty-three-year-old woman who has a rare disease that makes her look like a child, and who has killed in a similar fashion many times previously.

30. *Donnie Darko* ends with Donnie being killed in the plane crash that he appeared to avoid being killed in at the beginning of the film. If this were just another "he was dead the whole time" twist, it would not warrant a place on this list. What makes this one special is that he actually employs some nifty time travel and really strange metaphysics to bring about his own prior death.[1]

Appendix 2
Spoiler Horror Stories

Almost everybody has either spoiled something for someone else or had something spoiled for them. Usually, the
details are not all that interesting (someone reveals a
spoiler, someone gets angry, no one gets stabbed in the
chest), but sometimes the stories are just too good not to
share. Here are some real spoiler horror stories. The
names have been changed to protect the innocent (except
for the first one and the last one).

RICHARD (the author of this book) writes:

They say that confession is good for the soul, so I thought
I'd lead off with a time that I spoiled something for my
wife. She informed me that she had just begun reading
Jane Austen's *Emma*. Without thinking, I blurted out that
the Amy Heckerling film *Clueless* was based on *Emma*.
She shouted "Spoiler alert!" But that didn't stop me. I said
"I thought you knew that. You can tell that it is true because . . ." and then I proceeded to tell her all the characters in *Clueless* that were based on characters in *Emma*.
To which she responded that now she knows what happens to pretty much every character in *Emma*. It was the
spoiler that would not quit.

DELPHINE writes:

I have a couple of spoiler horror stories. The first one is from the film *The Jagged Edge*. In it a woman is attacked by a man with a mask on. At the end of the movie the woman is attacked again in the same manner. It seems to be the same man wearing the same mask, etc. The woman pulls the mask off and it was her husband all along. We were watching this film for the second time with my sister-in-law and a friend who hadn't seen it. Just after the first attack, the friends asks "What just happened?" My sister-in-law replies "Her husband attacked her." She ruined what was the absolute only secret of the whole film.

My second spoiler story is from the movie *Mask*. When I told a friend that I was going to see the film, she just blurted out "You know that when the boy in the movie complains of a headache at the end you know he is going to die." I was so bummed to hear this that I complained about this spoiler to a group of friends, but I neglected to check with them to see if they had seen the movie. They hadn't, so I spoiled it for them, too. This one was a double spoiler.

RUDOLPH writes:

I was a victim of a spoiler reveal. Not so long ago I was scrolling through my favorite social media sites—Facebook and Reddit. I was excited to watch *The Force Awakens*. Nearly every meme I saw informed me that Han Solo dies in the film. I would rather have learned this by watching the film.

CHAUNCEY writes:

I was taking a philosophy class. The topic of the course was the metaphysics of persistence. My professor (who may or may not be the author of this book) and another student began discussing the season finale of Season Two of *Westworld*, which had just aired maybe two weeks earlier (and I should point out, had nothing to do with persistence). My professor had just edited a book on *Westworld*, and he and the kid were pretty excited to discuss the finale. It seems like both of these guys should have known better (especially the one writing the book on spoilers). I wondered when either of them would ever shut up about it.

ERNIE writes:

I belong to a Facebook group called "Unappreciated Puns," so I thought no big thing. Then they posted puns related to the main characters who got killed in *Avengers: Infinity War*. It really just made me feel defeated. I was betrayed by puns.

NED writes:

I don't remember what season it was, but it was when it seemed like Glenn on the *The Walking Dead* died, but he didn't actually die. My then girlfriend told me that Glenn died. I told her "Dude, what are you doing? You can't spoil this for me!" Later when it turned out that he didn't actually die, she told me that, too. She managed to spoil this one twice.

TINA writes:

Grey's Anatomy is my absolute favorite series of all time. I always watch each episode when it first airs. One week I needed to record it on the DVR because I had a family dinner to attend while it was on, so I planned on watching it when I got home. I went to the dinner and on the ride home, I was browsing my Facebook account and I came across a post from a friend that said, "Oh my god! Derek died. Noooo!!!" I was devastated because that moment was the most shocking and terrible moment and episode of the whole series, and when I went home and watched the episode, it was ruined for me. I knew exactly what was coming and it didn't take effect on me like it would have if I hadn't previously found out.

SKEPPO writes:

Our family always reads together in the evenings. We select a book and take turns reading out loud from it. At one point we decided to read the *Harry Potter* books. My wife, who had read the series previously did most of the reading, since she was really good with the different voices. Unfortunately, her having read the series before led to her unintentionally revealing a slew of spoilers. A few pages before a major character dies, she would start to cry. We didn't always know who was going to die, when she started crying, but we knew that someone was going to die.

WANDA writes:

When I was younger I had never actually watched *Citizen Kane*, but I had watched a lot of cartoons as a child. One of them was *Pinky and the Brain*, which did a whole episode on *Citizen Kane*. This episode spoiled *Citizen Kane* for a whole generation of kids. Later in life when I finally got around to watching *Citizen Kane* I already knew what "Rosebud" referred to.

CLUBBER writes:

I really enjoy playing fantasy football. My sister, who lives in another state, and I enjoy this together. Often on Sunday afternoons I will call her to talk about how our teams are doing while we watch the games. Sometimes we are watching the same game. This is when things go badly. I watch on satellite tv, which contains a delay. My sister watches on cable, which doesn't have a delay (or has less of a delay; I don't really know how it works). Anyhow, she's always reacting to plays before they appear on my tv. I tell her not to do it, but she can't help herself. She just keeps shouting "touchdown" or "fumble" or "interception" or whatever, before I get to watch it for myself.

ESMERALDA writes:

I was watching the Academy Awards. I hit pause on the DVR so that I could fix myself a snack. While I was putting mustard on some bread, the results came across my phone app. That darned CNN spoiled the academy awards for me.

PENNY writes:

My spoiler story is from *Grey's Anatomy*, which is my favorite show. I went on Twitter and it was all over Twitter that the main character, Derek Shepherd, died after about ten seasons, and I hadn't seen the episode yet. Ugh!

LUCKY writes:

My spoiler is about *Game of Thrones*. I was scrolling through social media one day. My dad, who I don't talk to all that much, posted on social media how Jon Snow had died. It was only a couple of days after the episode premiered. I was pretty upset because I was really invested in *Game of Thrones* and Jon Snow is the best.

TAMALE JIM writes:

Whenever the game *Fallout 4* had just come out, my friends and I had a group chat going. One of my friends sent a meme to the group chat. At the top of the meme it had some funny stuff that had nothing to do with the game. It was just funny. At the bottom of the meme, though, there was a spoiler that told how the game ended. At the end of the game you find your son that you haven't seen in forever, since you've been in a vault frozen, and then you blow your son up!

DECLAN writes:

My spoiler horror story is not about a specific instance, but, rather, a thing that happens over and over. I get really bugged when I go to watch a film on Netflix, and just before the film begins they show you a trailer for that movie. That's the last time that you want to see a trailer for the film. Sometimes this happens in the theater too. Just before *Murder on the Orient Express*, they showed a trailer for *Murder on the Orient Express*. I was like "Nooooo! Not now, not now!" It's that phenomenon where they over-promote the movie.

FELICIA writes:

I watched *Game of Thrones* after my family had watched all of it. I was on some specific season, but my sister thought I was further along than I was.[2] So, she says "You know that Hodor dies?" I said "No, I don't know that!" I was so upset. Then I watched the episode where he dies. It was still just as upsetting, even though I knew what was going to happen, but instead, I was upset for the entire episode.

---

[2] As Bertrand Russell would undoubtedly have pointed out, of course she wasn't further along than she was!

BUCKY writes:

My father has the worst luck with spoilers. He is a huge college football fan. He almost always goes to the University of Utah home games, and when he can't he is careful to make sure no one tells him the result, since he watches later on DVR. A couple of years ago the Utes had a big game, and my father couldn't watch because he had other obligations. He avoided television and radio all day. He turned off alerts on his phone, and instructed everyone not to say anything to him. His plan had only one flaw. He was wearing his Utes jersey when the pizza delivery guy came to the door. Of course, the first thing out of the pizza guy's mouth was "Bummer about the Utes, huh?" Similar things have happened when relatives didn't get the message not to tell him the results.

BITSY AND WELDON write:

The spoiler that we are bringing up has to do with the sixth *Harry Potter* book. When it was to be released the lines to get the book were very long. A large coalition of jerks formed. These yahoos drove by bookstores yelling "Snape killed Dumbledore!" When news of this went viral, the stories about it on the Internet also to served to spoil the ending for a number of others. As near as I could tell, their sole motive for doing this was to be funny. One of us was one of those people who had the ending spoiled. It was not funny.

MISSOULA writes:

I was in the process of reading *The Hunger Games* series, and hadn't quite finished the books yet. My friend was under the impression that I had, because I told her I really enjoyed *The Hunger Games*, referring to the first book in the series, not the whole series. She thought I meant the whole series, so she revealed which characters die in the end, and that Katniss and Peeta end up together, which I didn't see coming at all. It made me really angry. I didn't know that the whole series was referred to as *The Hunger Games*, too

ROSABEL writes:

I watched the trailer for *Marley and Me*. It featured Owen Wilson and dogs. I thought it looked cute. I heard from someone before I went to see the film, that the dog dies at the end. It really turned me off. I haven't seen a movie since. This spoiler spoiled all movies for me. Maybe it was for the best that I didn't go to this one.

RICHARD (the author of this book) writes:

Finally, we have my very favorite spoiler horror story. This is not a story in which a spoiler is revealed (thank goodness—you'll see why momentarily), but, rather, a story in which a spoiler warning was the horror story. When my son, Henry, was six years-old, we took a family trip to France. We were flying out of New York City and heading to Dublin, where we had a brief layover. The flight attendents launched into their inflight safety spiel. When they got to the part about emergency landings and life vests, Henry began repeatedly shouting "Spoiler Alert!" Plenty of people found this amusing, but a number of the more nervous passengers were pretty freaked out. They wondered what he knew. It seemed to them to be a bad omen or some such. For some, it was a very long flight!

Appendix 3
The 100 Greatest
Philosophical Spoilers

THEODOR ADORNO: Art was much better a long time ago.

ANAXIMANDER OF MILETUS: Goodness, gracious, it all starts with great balls of fire.

G.E.M. ANSCOMBE: The road to Hell is paved with good intentionality.

ANSELM OF CANTERBURY: Necessarily there must exist a spoiler than which no greater spoiler can be conceived.

THOMAS AQUINAS: Divine revelation is mostly dispensed by Aristotle.

ARISTOTLE: All things said by Plato are wrong. The Theory of Forms is a thing said by Plato. Therefore, the Theory of Forms is wrong.

HANNAH ARENDT: Bring it on, Government!

MARY ASTELL: Educate women, and then watch them win debates.

AUGUSTINE OF HIPPO: Original sin is gonna get you.

AVERROES: Philosophy trumps scripture.

ALFRED JULES AYER: Spoilers can be verified and hence are not meaningless.

SIMONE DE BEAUVOIR: It takes a village to construct female identity.

JEREMY BENTHAM: Spread a little sunshine.

GEORGE BERKELEY: What you see is what you get.

SISSELA BOK: If you are in the public sphere, try not to lie.

GEORGE BOOLE: Aristotle was wrong about syllogisms.

F.H. BRADLEY: God can help you be the best darned you that you can be.

JUDITH BUTLER: If you want to be a particular gender, then act like it.

ALBERT CAMUS: It's absurd to try to reduce Camus's work to a single sentence.

RUDOLF CARNAP: If it can't be verified, it sucks.

MARGARET CAVENDISH: It's Alive!

CONFUCIUS: The Golden Rule is actually a Silver Rule.

NICOLAS COPERNICUS: What goes around comes around.

DEMOCRITUS: Ultimately everything is really small.

AUGUSTUS DE MORGAN: Every "or" is an "and" at heart (and *vice versa*).

RENÉ DESCARTES: Magic happens in the pineal gland.

FRED DRETSKE: It's probably a zebra, but one never knows.

DUNS SCOTUS: Essence is both existence and really weird.

ELISABETH OF BOHEMIA: Substance Dualism is for suckers.

EPICURUS: It's good to relax, perhaps with a nice snack.

EPICTETUS: Whatever happens, happens. Just roll with it.

EUCLID OF ALEXANDRIA: The longest distance from the point where you buy your tickets to the point where you purchase your popcorn is that winding line marked off by the red velvet ropes.

HARRY FRANKFURT: The Principle of Alternative Possibilities is bullshit!

EDMUND GETTIER: Know problem!

KURT GÖDEL: Logic, you don't complete me.

NELSON GOODMAN: In the future, some colors will be gruesome.

GEORG WILHELM FRIEDRICH HEGEL: Nothing is truly at odds with anything else; rather, everything is just on some big transcendent joy ride.

HERACLITUS OF EPHESUS: One can't spoil the same story twice.

MARTIN HEIDEGGER: Being is good, not by accident, but by *Dasein*.

HIPPOCRATES: If it *is* broke, you must fix it.

THOMAS HOBBES: Don't ever go camping, because in nature things really suck.

DAVID HUME: I don't believe in miracles. Awww, where you from, you sexy thing?

EDMUND HUSSERL: There are more things in consciousness, than are dreamt of in your natural philosophy, Horatio.

HYPATIA OF ALEXANDRIA: She contributed greatly to Ptolemy's work, just how much is unknown. Your Almagest is as good as mine.

LUCE IRIGARAY: Men and women are different.

FRANK JACKSON: There's something (different) about Mary.

WILLIAM JAMES: Truth is ultimately whatever will get you published.

IMMANUEL KANT: What if everyone did that? (I'm pretty sure he lifted this from his mother.)

SØREN KIERKEGAARD: Might as well jump.

CHRISTINE KORSGAARD: To know thyself, is to practically identify thyself.

SAUL KRIPKE: Things in France are exactly the length that they are.

GOTTFRIED WILLHELM LEIBNIZ: It's monads all the way down.

LAOZI: Gotta get back to (human) nature.

DAVID LEWIS: If it's possible, it's real.

JOHN LOCKE: The mind is a blank slate that eventually gets filled up with stuff, only some of which is real.

LUCRETIUS: Don't worry about death, you won't be there for it.

NICCOLÒ MACHIAVELLI: Whenever possible, be a total bastard.

Nicolas Malebranche: I didn't do it, God did it.

RUTH BARCAN MARCUS: Whatever Kripke said much later is true.

KARL MARX: Religion is totally dope.

ALEXIUS MEINONG: Yes, Virginia, there is a Santa Claus.

MICHEL DE MONTAIGNE: I don't know jack!

JOHN STUART MILL: If it makes you happy, it can't be that bad.

MONTESQUIEU: Power corrupts.

THOMAS NAGEL: Don't even think about what it is like to be a bat.

FRIEDRICH NIETZSCHE: What doesn't kill God makes him stronger, except something did kill him.

ROBERT NOZICK: None for all and all for none.

MARTHA NUSSBAUM: Good things break easily.

WILLIAM OF OCKHAM: Don't multiply spoilers unnecessarily.

PARMENIDES: It's all one big something, and whatever it is, it doesn't move much.

BLAISE PASCAL: I'll wager that you can guess this one.

PLATO: Philosopher kings!!! 'Nuff said.

PLOTINUS: There is just one thing, and it ain't a thing, and it ain't everything, either.

HILARY PUTNAM: Dude, you like totally might be in the Matrix.

PYRRHO OF ELIS: Don't worry, but don't exactly be happy either.

PYTHAGORAS OF SAMOS: Everything is made of math.

W.V. QUINE: Two dogmas walk into a bar . . .

JOHN RAWLS: All kinds of good stuff might happen, if you find yourself behind the right veil.

THOMAS REID: Skepticism bad, common sense good.

WILLIAM DAVID ROSS: Always let your conscience be your guide.

JEAN-JACQUES ROUSSEAU: Every child left behind.

BERTRAND RUSSELL: If you are a barber, there is a good chance that you will have to go to another town to get a decent shave.

GILBERT RYLE: Machines are not all that spooky.

JEAN-PAUL SARTRE: Other people are nauseating.

ARTHUR SCHOPENHAUER: It's best to neither desire nor act.

PETER SINGER: Be kind to your web-footed friends.

SOCRATES: I don't know anything, also know thyself, and if you can't pull off both of those simultaneously, just relax with a refreshing glass of ice-cold hemlock.

BARUCH SPINOZA: Everything is God (which, by the way comes as great news to my ego).

P.F. STRAWSON: I know what Russell was referring to, but he doesn't.

SUN TZU: Trick your enemy.

ALFRED TARSKI: Finally, the logicians and mathematicians get to talk about truth, too.

THALES OF MILETUS: You're gonna get wet.

JUDITH JARVIS THOMSON: Nine months is, frankly, just too long to be hooked up to a violinist (or any musician, for that matter!).

ALAN TURING: Computers can fool some of the people some of the time . . .

VOLTAIRE: Accentuate the negative, eliminate the positive.

MARY ANNE WARREN: Perhaps infanticide is not as bad as you think.

ALFRED NORTH WHITEHEAD: All of philosophy is either a footnote to Plato, or an over-used platitude about a footnote to Plato.

LUDWIG WITTGENSTEIN: Don't quit your day job, unless your day job is being a professional philosopher.

MARY WOLLSTONECRAFT: If you properly educate women, you just might give birth to a Frankenstein.

ZENO OF ELEA: Before you reveal a spoiler, you must reveal half a spoiler, and before that a quarter of a spoiler, and so on. Thus, it is impossible to spoil anything.

Index

THE
PRINCESS
BRIDE

AND PHILOSOPHY
INCONCEIVABLE!

EDITED BY RICHARD GREENE AND
RACHEL ROBISON-GREENE

*This book has not been prepared, authorized,
or endorsed by the creators or producers of
The Princess Bride*